"It's difficult to know what to say about this book, apart from the fact that it is insightful, accessible, refreshing, profound, and biblical. Oh, yes, and that in reading it my affections were reordered and restored, and I found myself desiring the glory of Christ far above and beyond my own."

Steve Timmis, Executive Director, Acts29

"While reading I was convicted of my tendency to crave glory and applause. Every chapter is laced with JR's vulnerability and honesty, while the hero of the book remains God, his glory, and his kingdom. This is a book I'll insist every member of my team reads to help us reject personal glory, embrace the discipline of obscurity, and spotlight Jesus alone."

Aaron Ivey, Worship Pastor, The Austin Stone, Austin, Texas

"There is nothing more native to the human experience than to want approval. We don't just seek it—we live for it! *Glory Hunger* shows us why we hunger for approval and points us to the only one who can satisfy that hunger."

Darrin Patrick, Lead Pastor, The Journey, St. Louis; Vice President, Acts 29; Chaplain, St. Louis Cardinals; author, *The Dude's Guide to Manhood.*

"A helpful meditation on the goodness of our search for glory, where it goes wrong, and how to set our hearts on the path to everlasting glory."

Bethany L. Jenkins, Founder and President, The Park Forum

"Hits the nail on the head about the condition of the human heart. In today's world of obsession with fame and of a "me first" mentality, Vassar delivers a timely message. Great food for thought and medicine for the soul."

Bryan Loritts, Lead Pastor, Fellowship Memphis, Memphis, Tennessee; author, *Right Color, Wrong Culture*

"A penetrating look behind the curtain of what drives everything we do in life. I love Vassar's discernment into the heart of man in *Glory Hunger.*"

Matt Carter, Pastor of Preaching, The Austin Stone Community Church, Austin, Texas; author, *The Real Win*

D0068452

"Vassar diagnoses the central problem of every human heart with the brilliance of a surgeon, but—even better—he shows us with pastoral wisdom and fatherly care the words that will heal us forever."

Jared C. Wilson, Pastor, Middletown Springs Community Church, Middletown Springs, Vermont; author, *Gospel Wakefulness* and *The Pastor's Justification*

"A great reminder of God's passion for his glory. My friend JR Vassar challenges our addiction to worldly glory and compels us to ascribe to Jesus the glory that he deserves. Read this book, reflect on its challenge, and apply it to your life."

Doug Logan Jr., Lead Pastor, Epiphany Fellowship of Camden, Camden, New Jersey

"JR does a magnificent job explaining the core reason we desire respect, status, approval, and praise: we bear the image of God, who exists to be glorified. *Glory Hunger* is an excellent resource to help us steward our natural attraction to glory. When the hierarchy of our loves is rightly ordered, with God occupying front and center, all other loves, desires, and ambitions find healthy expression."

Scott Sauls, Senior Pastor, Christ Presbyterian Church, Nashville, Tennessee; author, *Jesus Outside the Lines: A Way Forward for Those Who Are Tired of Taking Sides*

GLORY HUNGER

Foreword by
MATT CHANDLER

GL RY

O

HUNGER

God, the Gospel, and
Our Quest for Something More

JR Vassar

CROSSWAY
WHEATON, ILLINOIS

Glory Hunger: God, the Gospel, and Our Quest for Something More

Copyright © 2015 by Charles L. Vassar Jr.

Published by Crossway
      1300 Crescent Street
      Wheaton, Illinois 60187

Cover design: Erik Maldre

First printing 2015

Printed in the United States of America

Unless otherwise indicated, all Scripture quotations are from the ESV® Bible (*The Holy Bible, English Standard Version*®), copyright © 2001 by Crossway. 2011 Text Edition. Used by permission. All rights reserved.

All emphases in Scripture quotations have been added by the author.

Trade paperback ISBN: 978-1-4335-4010-3
ePub ISBN: 978-1-4335-4013-4
PDF ISBN: 978-1-4335-4011-0
Mobipocket ISBN: 978-1-4335-4012-7

Library of Congress Cataloging-in-Publication Data
Vassar, J R, 1973–
Glory hunger : God, the gospel, and our quest for something more / JR Vassar ; foreword by Matt Chandler.
      pages cm
   Includes bibliographical references and index.
   ISBN 978-1-4335-4010-3 (tp)
1. Christian life. 2. Hunger—Religious aspects—Christianity.
3. Fame—Religious aspects—Christianity. 4. Desire for God.
5. Glory of God—Christianity. I. Title.
BV4509.5.V38   2015
248.4—dc23   2014010883

Crossway is a publishing ministry of Good News Publishers.

VP   25   24   23   22   21   20   19   18   17   16   15
14   13   12   11   10   9   8   7   6   5   4   3   2   1

To Ginger,
spice of my life,
follower of Jesus,
supportive wife,
invested mother,
and hospitable friend

Contents

Foreword

I find in my heart an insidious desire to be recognized and applauded. I work hard, I have some natural giftings, and I want people to notice this and say something to me and to others about how awesome I am. Notice that I used the word *awesome* there. If I had typed the word *glorious*, then all of us would have raised an eyebrow. In fact, as I read over the sentence and replace the word *awesome* with *glorious*, I feel a sharp stab of conviction, and my legs feel weak, and I feel as though I am in danger. Glory is ultimately God's, and though I might reflect it, any glory I have is my creator's, not mine. JR is right when he says that we all possess a legitimate glory hunger. I feel it in me, and it's broken badly.

Here's the thing about my insidious desire and why I am writing the foreword to this book: I hate that the desire to be recognized and applauded is in me, and although it varies in intensity and frequency, I must constantly be aware of it so that I might, by the grace of God, suppress and confess it. In my saner moments I am well aware that I am fragile and that God has not made me the hinge upon which his kingdom will swing. But sin isn't sane. I know what the Bible says about the proud. I am almost haunted by John 3:30, which says, "He must increase, but I must decrease," and by Psalm 138:6, which says, "Though the LORD is high, he regards the lowly, but the haughty he knows from afar." I want the fight within me to be over. I want to be aware of the pull in my heart toward being self-exalting and therefore God-belittling.

I have learned in this fight that certain battles will be fought until Jesus, who won us all when he won the war, returns. That's what makes this book such a gem. It's ammunition for the battle that will rage in me again. At the time of writing this foreword, my heart is in a good place; it is tuned in, and my mind is crisp and clear about who God is. Right now I have a healthy picture of myself and my meager work ethic and giftings. I also know that it won't be long until a skirmish erupts again, and I will need the truth of God's Word and the insight of godly men like JR Vassar who are in the fight with us and have some expertise that will serve and help each of us as we seek to decrease while Jesus increases.

Matt Chandler

Introduction

Built for Glory

My oldest daughter, Neeley, will tell you that, to date, her greatest moment in life happened on the playground in the fifth grade. A few years have passed, and she is still talking about it. Admittedly, my daughter is not the most athletic kid, but this was her one shining moment. On this particular day, the physical education teacher scheduled a kickball game. Neeley was playing just behind second base. Toward the end of the game a student on the opposing team kicked a ball right to her. It was lifted sky-high, and Neeley, summoning all the courage she could in the moment, drifted directly under the ball, I'm sure with her eyes closed. It miraculously landed in her arms. She still relives that moment, but in her imaginative replay, all her friends pick her up on their shoulders and carry her around the playground chanting, "Nee-ley! Nee-ley! Nee-ley!"

Glory hunger. We all have it. It begins as kids, when we have visions similar to my daughter's of great exploits, with the attention and applause that accompany them. We want to stand out and feel significant, and we are terrified by the prospect of obscurity. We imagine heroic feats like winning the race, scoring the winning touchdown, or taking one deep in the bottom of the ninth with the bases loaded and down by three runs—full count, of course. No one ever dreams of giving up the homer, just of hitting it. Others grow up dreaming of taking the stage, starring in the lead role or winning *American Idol*. Little girls see themselves in every Disney flick and imagine one day being prized and swept off their feet by a handsome prince.

Maybe that doesn't describe you at all. You may never imagine yourself winning the race or securing the victory for your team or attracting the attention of a cheering crowd. You may be a shy wall-flower who hates the spotlight and shrinks from the attention. But that does not mean you are not hungry for glory. You may be just as glory hungry as the Olympic athlete. For you, perhaps the pursuit of glory is less about achieving exploits and more about avoiding embarrassment. Maybe for you, seizing glory means sidestepping humiliation. You don't care about winning the race and taking the podium; you just don't want to trip and come in last. The applause of the crowd is not the prize for you; the prize is avoiding their jeers.

A passion for praise or a fear of humiliation—it's all glory hunger. As we grow out of our childhood dreams, our glory hunger only intensifies and moves into more mature domains: social status, academic exploits, career advancement, wealth, marriage, and family. These all become means of "making it," and making it is an effort to satiate our glory hunger.

This glory hunger is not new. It is why ancient kings waged war and rode out into battle. It is captured in the epic poem *Beowulf*, where the sentiment of the warrior is, "Let whoever can, win glory before death." And glory he wins, even as he is dealt a mortal blow. To kings, death with glory is better than life without it. Tolkien depicts this in *The Lord of the Rings*. As his army at Helms Deep is outnumbered by the enemies of Isengard, King Theoden addresses his troops:

> Now is the hour come, Riders of the Mark, sons of Eorl! Foes and fire are before you, and your homes far behind. Yet, though you fight upon an alien field, the glory that you reap there shall be your own for ever. Oaths ye have taken: now fulfil them all, to lord and land and league of friendship![1]

For the ancient warrior, death was better than humiliation. Yet we are no different. We preserve this instinct in our figures of speech—"I was so embarrassed I wanted to die"—even though we don't really mean it. Embarrassing moments make us cringe. Even years later when we are all grown up and should be over them, their memory still brings a rush of red to our cheeks. No one wants a steady diet of humiliation. We are glory hungry.

We share this hunger not only with ancient kings but with God himself. *Glory* is a biblical term. The dominant words for *glory* in the biblical text are the Hebrew *kabod* in the Old Testament and the Greek *doxa* in the New Testament. Literally, the word *kabod* speaks of fatness. It carries the idea of being weighty or heavy. It can be used literally to speak of the size of a person or an object, but more often it carries the idea of significance. The point is not the girth of something but its greatness. In this sense, to be weighty is to be consequential or impressive, possessing grandness or splendor.

When the writers of Scripture speak of the "glory of God," they are communicating his incomparable greatness and beauty. God set his glory "above the heavens" (Ps. 8:1), and he is passionate about his glory. The Psalms are replete with commands to praise the Lord and to ascribe to the Lord the glory due his name. To give glory to something means to deem it impressive and to attribute worth to it as something that possesses significance and importance. It is right of God to command that we give him glory. He is more worthy and more impressive than anyone or anything, and ultimately he alone deserves worship. He is the glorious one, and when we truly come to grips with his glory and greatness, we can't help but respond with praise.

In fact, we are hardwired to ascribe glory and praise to what we deem impressive. We feel wonder over a breathtaking vista, or shock and awe when our bones are rattled by rolling thunder. Giving glory is a natural human response to witnessing greatness, which is why our world is infatuated with celebrities. We are addicted to greatness. And when we see it, we ascribe worth and value to it.

Our glory hunger is not just a desire to see and respond to greatness. It is a desire to possess greatness and have others respond to it. Deep down we have a desire not only to ascribe worth to an object but also to have others ascribe worth to us. We want to be perceived as impressive and be affirmed as significant and important. Deep down we want glory. And here is why: we were made for it. We were made for glory. This hunger for glory is universal because it's part of humanity's intended design. What we will see on the following pages is that something has gone horribly wrong to twist this legitimate longing. Though our glory hunger has made us slaves to the applause of people, God has built us for glory and intends to satiate our hunger for it.

1

Glory in a Garden

In January of 2005 my family and I moved to New York City. We were not there long, when I received a jury duty summons. Welcome to New York. I had never served on a jury but had read enough John Grisham and had seen enough *Law & Order* to know that this could be really thrilling. After going through the screening process, I was selected as juror number thirteen—the alternate. I was to sit through the entire trial and be prepared to weigh in on the verdict in case one of the twelve jurors got knocked off by a cartel member or got the flu. No one caught a bullet or a bug, so I sat through three days of trial and in the end was dismissed. I missed out on deliberating with the jury and handing down a verdict on an accused man.

During the ordeal, I watched the man on trial. His head was down during most of it, but occasionally he looked up at us, the jury of his supposed peers. I'm sure he was searching for some hint of hope in our eyes that we might declare him innocent. It also dawned on me that I'm not much different from that man. Though I don't have a criminal record, I sit on trial every day in the court of human opinion, craving a positive verdict to be handed down on me from a jury of my peers. I'm constantly stacking up evidence, trying to sway the court to bestow upon me its approval. I argue my case for people's acceptance and appreciation. I look to other people for any trace of hope or hint that I am perceived as important. I am hungry for recognition, affirmation, applause, and love—to hear a *yes* spoken over me by everyone, sometimes anyone. And I fear hearing a *no* spoken over my life. With this desire for approval and acceptance comes an accompanying fear of rejection. I despise the thought of being invisible, unappreciated, or unloved.

I'm glory hungry. We all are, and we have been since the beginning when our first parents were placed in the garden of Eden.

Adam and Eve were the crowning achievement of God's creation. That is a stunning statement when you consider what God made as a warm-up. Galaxies, quasar clusters spanning four billion light-years, stars and constellations, sun, moon, oceans, mountains, and vast canyons, all crescendo in the triune God saying, "Now, let's turn it up a notch and make something in our image."

God created Adam and Eve so together they might bear the Trinitarian image. He filled them with his breath, blessed them, and gave them commands that served as directives for their collective life with him. As image bearers, God commanded them to multiply, filling the earth with his image, and to subdue the earth by exercising dominion over it. With these commands came three colossal privileges that set them apart from the rest of creation.

First, they would relate to God in a unique way. Adam and Eve enjoyed an up-close-and-personal relationship with God. Every day, at sunset, God would visit them and invite them to take a walk in the cool breeze (Gen. 3:8). God was to Adam and Eve a father and intimate friend, a privilege they enjoyed as one made in God's image. They found their significance, purpose, and joy in belonging to him and being with him. God delighted in them, and they delighted in him in the unbroken fellowship of intimacy.

Second, they would reflect God. Adam and Eve must have been stunningly beautiful. Their proximity to God would have made them radiant. Similar to how Moses in later generations would commune with God face-to-face, absorbing the glow of God's glory and reflecting it to Israel (Ex. 34:29–35), Adam and Eve shone with the radiance of God's glory as they lived in a face-to-face relationship with him. Not only did they reflect the visible glory of God, but also they reflected his attributes as those made in his likeness. In their state of innocence they possessed uncorrupted goodness that made the beauty of God's holiness and love tangibly evident in their interactions with one another.

Third, they were to represent God, Adam serving as God's deputy with Eve by his side, together carrying out God's purposes for his creation. In Genesis 2:20 God delegates to Adam the responsibility of naming the animals. In the ancient Near East, to name something was to exercise control and authority over it, so by naming the animals, Adam was executing his rule over them. Adam and Eve were to cultivate the garden of God, creating culture and enhancing the beauty of all that God had made. As his image bearers they were set apart from the rest of creation and given unparalleled dignity and status. They were his intimate ones, precious and commissioned with divine purpose. These unique ones eclipsed any other work of God's hand. Their response was to live in humble gratitude to God, glorify God, and enjoy him for his perfections. They were to serve him as they carried out his directives for their lives. And as the scene closes in the first chapter of the Scriptures, God looks upon all he has made, Adam and Eve his proudest making, and hands down the verdict "very good."

Psalm 8 is a song that celebrates this moment in creation. It highlights God's special attention toward mankind as his pride and joy:

> When I look at your heavens, the work of your fingers,
>   the moon and the stars, which you have set in place,
> what is man that you are mindful of him,
>   and the son of man that you care for him?

Yet you have made him a little lower than the heavenly beings
 and crowned him with glory and honor.
You have given him dominion over the works of your hands;
 you have put all things under his feet,
all sheep and oxen,
 and also the beasts of the field,
the birds of the heavens, and the fish of the sea,
 whatever passes along the paths of the seas. (vv. 3–8)

In the garden God bestowed glory upon Adam and Eve. In spite of all the beauty and wonder put on display in the heavens, God's attention is riveted on the man and his wife. He set honor upon them, giving them an intimate place of prominence and purpose and voicing his affirmation over their lives.

Think of the greatest compliment you have ever been given. It might have been about your appearance or personality or some great accomplishment. Compliments do something to us. They bring a smile to our face and puff up our chest. They make us feel important. Now, imagine the explosion of joy and sense of worth that must have swelled up in the hearts of Adam and Eve as they hear, "Very good." It's one thing for your significant other to praise you for your appearance, or a colleague to compliment your work, but to have the God of the cosmos announce over the totality of your life and being, "You are very good!" is an incomparable compliment. What an amazing declaration. The *yes* of God, saying, "I approve of you! I delight in you! I am thrilled by you! I'm so glad that you are here and that you are mine!" What a verdict.

And Adam and Eve gloried in that verdict. It was the most important thing about them and the greatest thing that could be said of them. The end of Genesis 2 tells us that they were "naked and were not ashamed" (v. 25). In their state of innocence, with the pleasure of God over their lives and his approval ringing in their ears, they had nothing to hide and nothing to prove. As image bearers who related to God, reflected God, and represented God, they were the apple of his eye, and he was supreme in their hearts, and everything was very good.

This is the remarkable state we were created to live in—the glorious God crowning us with praise and approval as his image bearers. This is why there is a primal longing in all of us to be visible and feel valuable. We want to be lauded and loved. We were made to live in the privileged place of intimacy with God, reflecting the radiance of his glory, with everything under our feet. But things are not as they are supposed to be. Something has gone horribly wrong.

If the opening chapters of Genesis were put to a soundtrack, the music would shift to a dark and minor key in chapter 3. As the chapter opens we are made aware that something is amiss. A serpent suddenly appears, who is described as crafty. The New Testament unmasks this Serpent as our great enemy, Satan (Rev. 12:9). In his hatred for God, Satan went after those made in God's image, the part of creation that mattered most to God.

He approached Eve, and Eve engaged him in conversation. Satan sought to discredit God and convince Eve that God was somehow holding out on her. In spite of her glorious position and the crown that God had placed upon her, she began to long for a promotion. She could be more than a creature made in the image of God; she could become just like God. If she took of the forbidden fruit, she could have open eyes and Godlike discernment, knowing the difference between good and evil. Eve began to believe that she could have a glory—a glory of her own—that surpassed what had been bestowed upon her.

At the heart of this temptation was the pursuit of radical independence from God and rogue glory. Eve bit on the temptation and led Adam to join her in this treason, reaching for Godlike status.

Immediately Satan's promise was realized. Their eyes were opened, and they saw the sharp distinction between good and evil—God was good, and they were evil. Their attempt to secure glory independent of God left them in a foreign state of guilt. The ones who held their heads high, crowned with the "very good" of God, now hung their heads in shame.

The rest of the chapter shows us that though Adam and Eve maintained the image of God, there was a tragic diminishing of that image and a loss of the glory that had crowned them. Instead of relating to God in intimate love and joyful dependence, they hid from God in shame and fear. God banished them from the garden, no longer walking with them in intimate face-to-face fellowship (Gen. 3:24). Instead of reflecting the beauty of God's perfections, they had become corrupt in their nature. Augustine of Hippo described their new, fallen condition as *incurvatus in se*, a turning in on oneself.

Adam and Eve curved inward and were no longer living toward God and one another in love but were bent on living for themselves. Their relationship with one another had become marked by a selfish grasp and struggle for power, the woman desiring the husband's position and the husband ruling over his wife (v. 16). The great privilege of representing God in creation was retained but frustrated by the disintegration of creation. Filling the earth and subduing it was now to be a painful, sorrowful, and difficult process (vv. 16–18). They suffered the loss of greatness, becoming weak and susceptible to their environment, and they would now experience the greatest of all inglorious events: death. The very ground that Adam was to subdue as God's representative would now subdue him as he returned to the dust from which he had been formed (v. 19). All creation, including Adam and Eve, had fallen under the curse of God.

The "very good" was vandalized, and Adam and Eve experienced the fracturing of the image of God within them. They were still valuable and loved as God's creation, possessing indescribable dignity and worth, but they had lost what their hearts were made to possess. God's gavel came down with a new verdict. They were guilty, cursed, alienated, exiled, and sentenced to death. They lost the smile and commendation of God and were separated from him by their willful rebellion.

This is the world we were born into. We were made God's image bearers, having intrinsic dignity and worth. We are not worthless or colossal wastes of space. Humans possess profound significance and should value life, our own and everyone's. But, what we were made to be and experience was tragically lost by our first parents when they sinned. We have joined them in that rebellion and share their guilt. The Scripture tells us in Romans 3:23 that all have sinned and continually fall short of the glory of God. We are cut off from the present glory that God intends for us, because of our rebellion. As his image bearers we were made to walk with him in intimate friendship, but we are alienated from him. We were made to hear the commendation of God spoken over us, but we are condemned before God. The beauty we were made to reflect is obscured by our inner corruption. And the greatness of ruling over creation with God is frustrated by our weaknesses, suffering, and death. Our greatest need is to have that glory restored to us. Deep down, it is the unnamed ache of every life. We need to have his commendation over us, his image renewed in us, and greatness reclaimed for us.

That is the legitimate glory hunger we all possess—to be restored to a glorious image and crowned with honor by God. Every glory-hunger pain we have for approval, acceptance, or achievement betrays a greater pain that exists in all of us. Our craving to be visible and valuable to people is really a legitimate and primal pang for what we are meant to have with the ultimate person. Glory hunger is the passion and ache we are born with to have that "very good" spoken over our lives. You can see that ache in the heart of every little boy who says, "Daddy, aren't I fast?" Or in little girls who say, "Daddy, am I pretty?" We never grow out of it. We exhaust ourselves for the A, the starting position on the team, or the corner office so that we will know in our eyes and in everyone else's that we are very good.

And though it is a legitimate hunger, it has illegitimate and idolatrous expressions. We attempt to satiate that hunger in futile ways by creating an image for ourselves that others will assess as "very good." Just as Adam and Eve sewed fig leaves together to cover up their lost glory, we continue to sew fig leaves in hopes of compensating for our lost glory. We hope to be praised for the fig leaves, but fig leaves wither, and the praise is never enough. We think if we can string together enough accolades, accomplishments, possessions, beauty, physique, intelligence, or exploits that we will build an image upon which the court of human opinion might render a positive verdict and satisfy the glory hunger that gnaws at us.

One of the privileges of pastoring in New York City was regularly receiving the ministry of Tim Keller. One of his classic illustrations deals with our glory hunger. In the movie *Rocky*, Rocky Balboa is talking to his future wife, Adrian, about the impossibility of beating the champion Apollo Creed. Rocky knows he can't win, so his goal is to survive, to go the distance and to stand when the final bell rings. For Rocky, this is the one thing that will prove to him and to everyone else that he isn't "just another bum from the neighborhood."

We are glory deficient and feel it. And no accomplishment or airbrushing will ever make up the deficit. Our passion to be visible and valuable, to create an unfading image that will carry a lasting verdict of very good, is beyond our reach. And now the natural trajectory of fallen humanity is to seek that lost glory in the praises and affirmation of other people. Like the builders at the Tower of Babel of Genesis 11, who literally tried to build a name for themselves by constructing something great that would gain them fame, we strive to save ourselves from a felt insignificance by making a name for ourselves. We construct an image and build up a reputation so that we will know, along with everyone else, that we aren't just another bum in the universe.

Yet there is hope. Even in the judgment God pronounces upon Adam and Eve, there is a promise that one is coming who will crush the head of the Serpent and overturn this tragic situation (Gen. 3:16). God will make a way to renew his commendation over us, restore his image in us, and reclaim lost greatness for us. But our reaching for glory will not bring about this transformation. No, God will come to us, and it will be his work, not ours. It is reaching that robbed us of this glory in the first place. Grasping for glory is the one sure way to miss it.

2

Broken Buddhas

I like being liked. I'm not referring to the affirmation of a Facebook post; I'm referring to the affirmation of my person. The first time I read C. S. Lewis's essay "The Inner Ring," I felt like Uncle Jack was writing it for me. Lewis addresses our desire to be on "the inside." In classic Lewis fashion, he exposes our heart's desire to be liked and admitted into exclusive circles that we believe will give us identity, place, and significance. Lewis explains how we work hard to gain admittance into those circles:

> Men tell not only their wives but themselves that it is a hardship to stay late at the office or the school on some bit of important extra work which they have been let in for because they and So-and-so and the two others are the only people left in the place who really know how things are run. But it is not quite true. It is a terrible bore, of course, when old Fatty Smithson draws you aside and whispers, "Look here, we've got to get you in on this examination somehow" or "Charles and I saw at once that you've got to be on this committee." A terrible bore . . . ah, but how much more terrible if you were left out! It is tiring and unhealthy to lose your Saturday afternoons, but to have them free because you don't matter, that is much worse.[2]

I want to matter. We all do. As children on the playground, we feared being picked last for our lack of popularity or athletic prowess. We wanted to be wanted and to feel the approval of peers. Not much changes. We rarely get over the pursuit of popularity. It is not a teenage problem; it is a human problem. As grown men and women, we flinch at being overlooked or unwanted because we don't carry enough value in the eyes of those picking the teams. We want to be spoken well of and admired. We want glory. This is the residue of God's original design, his glorious image stamped upon us, yet shattered by sin. Our ache for glory is the Genesis memory of our original condition and God's original commendation lost in an act of treason. The fall brought about a tragic diminishing of glory, a vandalism of the "very good" once openly announced over innocent image bearers. Now, we are all born outsiders, east of Eden, and we feel it. Our pursuit of significance is at its deepest level a longing to recapture what was lost in the fall.

In John 12:42–43 we read a tragic account of glory-hungry people seeking their place in the inner ring. A number of religious leaders had come to believe in Jesus. However, there were some serious consequences to confessing it. If they went public with their belief in him, it would mean being put out of the synagogue. In that culture, to be removed from the synagogue was to lose face. It meant losing public standing and being stripped of social capital. Being removed from the synagogue meant being designated an outsider. Once you lost your honor and became an outsider, it was almost impossible to regain that honor and make your way back inside. John gives us a glimpse of the inner workings of their hearts:

> Many even of the authorities believed in him, but for fear of the Pharisees they did not confess it, so that they would not be put out of the synagogue; for they loved the glory that comes from man more than the glory that comes from God. (John 12:42–43)

Those men were motivated by a hunger for glory. John uses emotive language. They *loved* the glory that comes from men. Their hearts were fixated upon it. Their affections were awakened to the approval of other people. They measured their actions by it. They choreographed and timed their steps in such a way as to secure it. They did what was required to stay in the favor of a first-century Jewish culture—they denied Jesus and maintained their status in the synagogue. It was not worth confessing Jesus if it meant jeopardizing their place in the inner ring. So, to preserve the dominant culture's verdict of "very good" over their life, they maintained a culturally required image.

We are not much different from the people of John 12. If we are honest, our hearts are desperate for the praise of people. We desire to be insiders. We work hard to construct and maintain an image that we believe will impress others, earn their approval, and give us a sense of significance. We want to escape shame and shine with glory.

Think of all the ways this shows up in our culture and in our lives. We obsess over our appearance. Our culture stresses about weight, shape, and style, spending billions on efforts to enhance our beauty and bodies. When we are not obsessing over our physical image, we are tweaking our social image via social media so as to present an enviable life to those who may be watching. Our attempts to inflate our image as good parents lead us to expect too much from our children and crush them under those expectations. We exhaust ourselves chasing achievements we believe will win us self-respect and the admiration of others. Think of how over-committed we get because of the fear of disappointing someone by saying no. We cave to peer pressure and people pleasing, or we just hide, so we can avoid the pain of rejection. And when our love for the praise of people is at its worst, we refuse to confess Jesus and live out our faith convictions, fearing we will be branded as narrow-minded bigots standing in the way of cultural progress.

We often do whatever it takes to maintain our place in the cultural synagogue.

During my senior year of high school, I joined the drama team. On the first day of class we were given a terrifying assignment. Each student was required to stand in front of the class for one minute and do nothing but stare at the audience. We were not allowed to talk, make facial expressions, look down, or look away. We had to look our audience in the eye. It was the longest minute of my life. Most of us felt so uncomfortable that we ended up doing something silly to compensate for our insecurity of standing there with all eyes on us.

Loving the glory that comes from man is like that. It creates a life of bondage lived under the approving or disapproving gaze of people. It is as if we can feel the stares of others bearing down on us, forcing us to perform in hopes of their applause. Life feels like one big audition with the world as our audience and judge, and we just want to be liked.

In his book *When People Are Big and God Is Small*, Ed Welch points out that the love for the glory that comes from man comes down ultimately to "needing something from other people."[3] We need their approval, their love, their affirmation, and their attention to save us from our sense of insignificance and bestow value upon us. Receiving it becomes an idol. When we need others in this way, the result is bondage; our life is lived under the control of other people and their opinions of us. The idol of the glory that comes from man can own us like no other idol. It can tell us how to think, what to feel, how to act, what to wear, and when to laugh. As a pastor, I have counseled people who have crossed boundaries they had never imagined simply to gain or keep the approval of others. Whether it's drowning in debt because they made purchases to keep up with the people they wanted to impress, or drowning in guilt after moments of moral compromise motivated by preserving another's affections for them, people do regrettable things from a desire to be visible and feel valuable.

The glory hunger that John describes in his Gospel is an element of the fear of man: an excessive concern about people's opinions of us and a desire for their acceptance. It is the hunger for human approval and the fear of rejection. The fear of man is an intemperate desire to be accepted by people, with an accompanying fear of being rejected or victimized. When we are living under the fear of man, we calculate our behavior to gain the admiration of others, and we are careful to act in ways that will not put that admiration at risk. The desire for the respect and admiration of others and the accompanying desire to avoid the pain of rejection are normal and legitimate. They often keep us from sinful, destructive, shameful behavior.

There are a lot of things I have avoided because I did not want to get hurt, look like an idiot, or disappoint people I care about. I've never played chicken in a car, been drunk, or worn spandex. In that sense, the desires for respect and avoiding rejection can be good, but when the desires go unmet, or the fears are actualized, there is pain. We know this by experience. It hurts to be made fun of or to be fired. When the desires are met and the fears are escaped, there is happiness and a sense of pleasure, such as when we are awarded for an achievement or are asked for our hand in marriage. The problem is when these natural and legitimate desires become inordinate or excessive and controlling. When they loom too large in our hearts, we become consumed about what people think about us and have an excessive fixation on people's opinions, even if we don't know them. We feel we *need* the approval of someone or anyone, and we can't bear the thought of rejection.

My family moved to New York City in the dead of winter. My

oldest daughter was five at that time and was a social butterfly, but she had a hard time connecting with other children. Few families hang out in city parks when it is bitterly cold. After a couple of months of sporadic interaction with children, she began to grow lonely. Finally, we got a little reprieve from the cold, so I took my daughter to a park near our apartment. There was a group of children about her age climbing and playing on a large snow pile, so off she went to play. One by one the children left the park until my daughter and one other child, with long, flowing, blonde hair and an obvious adventurous spirit, were the only ones left.

When it was time for us to go, Neeley came running up to me, yelling, "Daddy, I made a friend!"

So, I asked her, "Did you get the kid's name?"

She shook her head no, so I encouraged her, "Go get the kid's name!"

Neeley ran across the playground and struck up a conversation with the child. A few seconds later she yelled at me from across the park, "Daddy, her name is David! And she's a boy!"

I'm ashamed to say it now, but I was embarrassed. The boy's father was standing nearby, and though I did not know him, I cared what he thought about me and what his son thought about my daughter. At the time, we were lonely and hungry for friendship. We were living in a new culture trying to learn all the cultural rules in order to win people's acceptance. We were doing our best to avoid any missteps that might cost us favor with others. I wanted this father and his son to like us, and somehow I thought this snafu put that in jeopardy.

That is a mild example, but it is not a mild struggle. Our hearts are often ruled by the fear of breaking cultural rules, which might jeopardize our place in the culture.

This hunger for the glory that comes from man is so insidious that it makes its way into even the most sacred of activities and taints the motivations of nearly every action. In Jesus's famous Sermon on the Mount, he tells people enamored by the religious celebrities of the day not to be like those who practiced their righteousness with the purpose of being seen and praised for it. Jesus refers to those who engaged in religious activities to increase their clout with others as "hypocrites." The Greek word translated "hypocrite" carries the sense of a play actor or a pretender. Praying, giving, and fasting can become public performances with the hope of standing out and being admired. Jesus knows that our temptation is to see life as a stage and the watching world as our audience. Even the most righteous acts can be done with one eye on God and the other eye on people, hoping they see that one eye on God and admire us for it.

As a minister, I have wrestled with that from the beginning of my ministry. I went to a Baptist university where the quickest way to gain clout on campus was to be visibly committed to Jesus. On some college campuses, the temptation is to morally compromise to fit in. Where I went to school, the temptation was to manufacture godliness to fit in. And many people did. Some students slept in on Sunday and missed out on worshiping with the local church, but in an attempt to maintain their image as good, churchgoing Christians, they would dress in their church clothes before making their way to the university cafeteria. They wanted to be seen as righteous for the sake of their image and reputation on the campus. Personally, as a young college student I had a sincere desire to follow Jesus, but I had a near equal desire for everyone to admire me for following Jesus. I wanted to live a righteous life, and I wanted to be seen and esteemed for the righteous life I lived. I wanted to serve Jesus, and I wanted to stand out for my service to Jesus.

During my freshman year of college I was occasionally invited to my home church to speak to our youth group on Sunday mornings. I preached the gospel and invited students to place their faith in Jesus, yet no students responded to my messages. Then the student pastor asked if I had any friends at college who might also come and preach to the students. To be honest, it stung me a little to be benched. When a friend did come to preach one Sunday, eleven students placed their faith in Jesus. I remember weeping afterward. My friend understood my emotion as a sign of my compassion for the students and my joy over seeing them come to saving faith. There was truth to that, but it was not all true—I was jealous. I wanted God to do great things, but I wanted him to do those great things through me. And I wanted everyone *to know* he did those great things through me. I wanted to stand out. I wanted to be told how gifted I was and patted on the back and praised for my ministry success. I wanted glory that comes from people, even if it meant stealing it from God. Two decades later I still fight the hunger to be esteemed for the gifts God has given me. I'm not much different from the people of John 12:42. I'm glory hungry.

As we considered in the previous chapter, this glory hunger is the pangs of a glory deficiency we all feel as a result of the fall. We were made in the image of God, possessing privilege and greatness unmatched in all of creation. But because the first humans, Adam and Eve, sought glory independently of God and so introduced sin into the world, that image is vandalized in their lineage. We don't perfectly reflect the glory of God. In our natural-born condition, we are no longer properly related to God. We are alienated from him and under his condemnation. As those born into Adam's family, with a nature curved in on itself and our backs to God, the natural trajectory of humanity is to reconstruct a substitute image in hopes of recapturing a lost glory and securing the approval of other people as a substitute for the approval of God.

The insanity in all of this is that *everyone* has this glory deficiency. Those we look to for affirmation are just as glory starved as we are. As praiseworthy and powerful as they seem, if we look deep enough, we discover that those we admire and whose approval we long for are no better off. They too are weak, flawed, fearful, and insecure. They are members of this fallen human race, exhausting themselves to be good enough to win the praise of a watching world.

Some of the most famous people of our day are courageous enough to admit it. In October of 2013, a *CNN Entertainment* article cited the fear and insecurity of several celebrities, many who are cultural icons. Meryl Streep was quoted as once telling *Oprah* magazine, "I say to myself, 'I don't know how to act—and why does anybody want to look at me on-screen anymore?' . . . Lots of actors feel that way. What gives you strength is also your weakness—your raging insecurity."[4] The stunningly beautiful Megan Fox was quoted in an interview with *Cosmopolitan* magazine: "I'm very confident in how I project my personality. But in terms of how I look, I'm completely, hysterically insecure. I'm self-loathing, introverted and neurotic."[5] Even the ever-confident and sensual Beyoncé confessed in her HBO documentary, "People see celebrities, and they have money and fame, but I'm a human being. I cry, and I get scared, and I get nervous, just like everyone else."[6] Just like everyone else. Just like your friends, your boss, your relatives, your next-door neighbor, that stranger on the street, or anyone else whose approval you crave. We are all glory deficient.

In 2000 I had the great privilege of ministering in Myanmar for two weeks. We were there to train indigenous pastors, but due to some governmental pressures we spent almost all of our time in the work of prayer walking. One day we were prayer walking through a large Buddhist temple, when I witnessed something heartbreaking.

A large number of people, very poor and desperate, were bowing down to a large golden Buddha. They were stuffing what seemed to be the last of their money into the treasury box and kneeling in prayer, hoping to secure a blessing from the Buddha. On the other side of the large golden idol, scaffolding had been built. The Buddha had begun to deteriorate, and a group of workers was diligently repairing the broken Buddha. I took in the scene. Broken people were bowing down to a broken Buddha asking the broken Buddha to fix their broken lives while someone else fixed the broken Buddha. The insanity and despair of it all hit me. We are no different from them. We are broken people looking to other broken people to fix our broken lives. We are glory-deficient people looking to other glory-deficient people to supply us with glory. Looking to other people to provide for us what they lack themselves is a fool's errand. It is futile to look to other glory-hungry people to fully satisfy our glory hunger, and doing so leaves our souls empty.

It is important to see in John 12 that John does not rebuke the officials for loving glory. The problem was not that they had an ache for affirmation and approval. John does not rebuke them for wanting to be on the inside. It's a natural and normal desire to want to be liked. The problem is who they were looking to for that affirmation and approval. They were fighting to be in the wrong inner ring. The tragedy is that they tried to satiate their glory hunger with an inadequate glory. They were looking to other glory-hungry people to satisfy their appetite for glory.

But there is a superior glory that can be conferred upon us, which is sufficient. There is a glory that comes from God, a glory we were made for, a glory that was lost but can be restored to us. The shock of John 12 is that those glory seekers had that glory available to them, but they were settling for a cheap substitute. They could have had the glory that comes from God, but they wanted the approval of old Fatty Smithson. Just like Adam and Eve, they traded the glory that comes from God for one they grasped and came up empty.

There is a glory available to us that we are to love, long for, and seek. It is right and legitimate to hunger for it. It is the glory that comes from God, and it is given to us in the gospel of his Son.

3

The End of the Sisyphus Cycle

My parents were kind enough to bequeath me a metabolism slower than a chess match. I did not ask for that. We don't have a say in those matters, nor do we have a say in the biological family we are born into. We might have chosen a different one if we could, but the truth is that the choice was out of our hands. Nor do we determine our genes, DNA, or natural talents. If we could, I would have chosen to be tall, fast, athletic, and naturally toned. As it is, I possess none of those traits, and neither did my parents. We can blame those kinds of things primarily on our biological family tree. The roots of that tree determine the fruits of our features. We reflect our biological fathers.

Spiritually, we are born with Adam as our father. After his tragic fall, he fathered a race "in his own likeness, after his image" (Gen. 5:3). When Adam sinned, he fell from the heights of glory. He incurred the condemnation of God, his nature was corrupted, and he lost the greatness he originally possessed. Through his sinful act, he brought this tragic loss on the entire human race (Rom. 5:12). We are in his lineage. We share his spiritual features. We are the branches of his family tree. Adam serves as the root of that tree and determines the fruit of the features of our inner life. As his children who have his blood coursing through our veins, we share his condemnation and corruption, and we too lack the greatness God intended for humanity.

We feel our condemnation. Deep down we know we are wrong, but we want to be right. We point fingers, shift blame, and justify ourselves because the pain of a soiled record and a condemning conscience is too much to bear. We feel our corruption, embarrassed over the things we are capable of. And we feel the loss of the dominion that was originally given to Adam in the fact that we are racked with a litany of limitations and failures. In light of the fact that we were made to rule over all creation (Ps. 8:6–8), our accomplishments don't quite scratch our itch for greatness, but we keep trying. Our glory hunger is the unrelenting fight to overcome this shame and recover the goodness and greatness that Adam lost.

I liken this struggle for the recovery of glory to what is sometimes called the "Sisyphus cycle." Sisyphus was a king in Greek mythology who was condemned by the gods to spend eternity pushing a large boulder up a steep hill. But it was an exercise in futility, since every time he reached the top of the hill, the large stone rolled back down to the bottom. When we are driven to recover glory for ourselves, it is like pushing a large boulder of our own goodness and greatness up an insurmountable hill. We struggle and strive in our attempts to feel good about ourselves by complying to our own moral code. We push and plod in our attempts to make everyone else feel good about us by meeting the cultural expectations for greatness. But we never quite make it over the top of the hill. We inevitably embarrass ourselves by failing to meet our own standards and by failing to embody the cultural values of successful, sexy, and cool. With every failure, the stone rolls back down to the bottom of the hill, and we don't feel good or great. So we start pushing the stone up the hill one more time. It is exhausting.

There is a way to be finally free from the vicious Sisyphus cycle.

But this freedom will not come by you and me climbing our own hills. We will find our glory hunger satisfied and the Sisyphus cycle broken by another, who heroically climbed the ultimate hill for us. Jesus, through his holy life, substitutionary death, and bodily resurrection has secured for us all the goodness and greatness for which our hearts ache. Our longing for the recovery of glory is met finally and fully in Jesus's work on the cross. His hill was Golgotha. He climbed it and heroically won back for us what Adam lost.

Our Approval Secured

Jesus was the only one since Adam's fall to be free of guilt and condemnation. He was the Son of God, born of a virgin and free from Adam's corruption. Jesus was without sin (Heb. 4:15) and always did what was pleasing to the Father (John 8:29). At his baptism the Father's voice spoke from heaven, "This is my beloved Son, with whom I am well pleased" (Matt. 3:17). Jesus asked his accusers, "Which one of you convicts me of sin?" (John 8:46). No one could, yet he died like a common criminal. The Jewish leaders condemned Jesus, and the Roman governor Pilate sentenced him to die by crucifixion. Yet it was ultimately God's plan. Though sinful people carried it out, the death of Jesus was ultimately God's intent (Acts 2:23).

In 2 Corinthians 5:21 Paul tells us what God accomplished in Jesus's death: "For our sake he made him to be sin who knew no sin, so that in him we might become the righteousness of God." By the cross of his Son, God made it possible for us to regain the standing and status that Adam lost for us. Jesus became our sin and bore our curse so that we could become his righteousness and know the blessing of God. The Father held his Son legally liable for our sins, and Jesus paid for them in his death on the cross. In a glorious exchange, Jesus's perfect obedience is credited to those who trust in him, and they are declared righteous. God took an eternity of what we deserved, bound it up into a moment, and unleashed it on his Son so he could spare us and give us an eternity of what we don't deserve. God looked upon Jesus as though he lived my life so that he could look upon me as though I lived Jesus's life. At the cross, the only commendable one became the condemned one, so that the condemned ones could become the commendable ones. Jesus removes our condemnation from us, bearing it himself. Now, for those who are in Christ, there is no condemnation before God but only the commendation of God.

I first began to understand the doctrine of justification by faith in my early college days. Poring over the Scriptures in my dorm room, my mind marveled and my heart sang over the fact that God had declared me righteous in his sight solely by faith in Jesus, apart from any work of my own and apart from my actual condition. Looking back, I now know I was starting to grasp what is clearly and succinctly laid out in the Heidelberg Catechism:

Q. How are you righteous before God?
A. Only by true faith in Jesus Christ. Although my conscience accuses me that I have grievously sinned against all God's commandments, have never kept any of them, and am still inclined to all evil, yet God, without any merit of my own, out of mere grace, imputes to me the perfect satisfaction, righteousness, and holiness of Christ. He grants these to me as if I had never had nor committed any sin, and as if I myself had accomplished all the obedience which Christ has rendered for me, if only I accept this gift with a believing heart.[7]

In other words, to be justified by God means that God sees me in Jesus, "just as if I had never sinned; just as if I had always obeyed." God considers me in Christ as having met all his expectations and fulfilled all his demands. Since I am "in Christ," I am not condemned by God; rather, I am loved, approved, and affirmed. This truth of justification is why the apostle Paul could say to the Corinthians:

> But with me it is a very small thing that I should be judged by you or by any human court. In fact, I do not even judge myself. For I am not aware of anything against myself, but I am not thereby acquitted. It is the Lord who judges me. (1 Cor. 4:3–4)

In other words, I'm not defined by how good I feel about myself or how good another feels about me. I'm not even defined by how good I really am or am not. I'm defined by what the Lord says about me. The Lord is my judge, and he has justified me. He has declared me righteous in his court and set his love and affirmation upon me forever.

Whether we have acknowledged it or not, this is the glory we want. Throughout our entire lives we have been seeking a positive verdict in the courtrooms of human opinion. Every courtroom in which you and I secure a positive verdict eventually gets trumped by a higher court, and then we exert all our energy for the favor of that higher court. I tight-rolled my jeans in the seventh grade for a middle-school courtroom. I worked hard at athletics for a high-school courtroom, and with every ground ball that went through my legs I lost the trial. I graduated from high school and college, and the courtrooms kept changing and getting more sophisticated and complicated. The demands of achievement and appearance became harder to attain. All along the way, I found (and find) myself living in a courtroom struggling to prove my case and be commended.

I'm guessing you have (and do) too. Maybe it was the courtroom of your parents, and you just wanted to hear your dad's verdict of "I'm proud of you." Maybe you're living for the verdict of a boss or a spouse or a social circle, and the best you can hope for is a hung jury. All these courts are shadows of the highest court. Our desire for a positive verdict in human courts is the surface rumbling of our deepest need for the ultimate verdict that comes down from the ultimate court.

God put in your heart this need to be justified, and until you are able to stand before him justified, with the verdict of "fully loved and fully accepted," you will never be truly free from all the lower courts you are living for. Until the opinion of the one who matters most actually matters most to you, you will never be free from your unrelenting glory hunger.

This is not legal fiction, a make-believe world in which we pretend we are okay. It is not a judicial act of God in which he coldly declares us righteous against his better judgment or wishes. It is the most real thing about us if we are in Jesus, and it is relational. God delights to credit us with the righteousness of Jesus and gladly adopts us in that righteousness as sons and daughters whom he loves and in whom he delights. We see the power of this as we eavesdrop on Jesus's prayer to the Father that led up to his crucifixion:

> The glory that you have given me I have given to them, that they may be one even as we are one, I in them and you in me, that they may become perfectly one, so that the world may know that you sent me and loved them even as you loved me. (John 17:22–23)

The last line of that request is staggering. Jesus was saying that because of his work at the cross, all who believe in him will be brought into a relationship with God and have him as their Father. As his children in Jesus, the Father loves us with the same commitment and joy with which he loves his own dear, eternal Son. He takes pleasure in his justified ones like he takes pleasure in Jesus. How he feels about Jesus is how he feels about those who are in Jesus. Just like God spoke over his Son at his baptism, "You are my beloved Son; with you I am well pleased" (Mark 1:11), he speaks over his adopted sons and daughters and says to us, "I claim you as my child, and I find happiness in you." And the Holy Spirit wants to convince us more and more of that reality and satisfy our hearts with it (Rom. 8:16). Jesus has won that glorious status for us, and the weight of it has the power to satisfy us like nothing else. I love how C. S. Lewis describes God's posture toward those in Christ:

> The promise of glory is the promise, almost incredible and only possible because of the work of Christ, that some of us, that any of us who really chooses . . . shall find approval, shall please God. To please God . . . to be a real ingredient in the divine happiness . . . to be loved by God, not merely pitied, but delighted in as an artist delights in his work or a father in a son—it seems impossible, a weight or burden of glory which our thoughts can hardly sustain. But it is so.[8]

Jesus has removed our condemnation and made us objects of God's delight, ingredients in the Father's happiness. I must admit that in the past I have cringed when others have spoken of God in highly emotional terms. I have been uncomfortable with songs and sermons that I felt made God look sappy. But after a recent encounter with God, that changed. At the time, my wife and I were struggling with fear in an area of our lives. We were praying late one night, and I began to reflect on the love of God. As I prayed, I had clear images in my mind of my interaction with my children. In that moment, I recalled the numerous times I have gone into their rooms while they sleep, stroked their hair, smiled over them, and whispered in their ear how much I love them.

As I prayed with my wife that night, I sensed in my heart that God was interrogating me. It seemed as if he were asking me, "Do you think you are a more tender father than I am? Are you more affectionate toward your children than I am toward mine? Is your heart more capable of delighting in your kids than my heart is capable of delighting in mine?" I was overwhelmed as I sensed the reality of God's love. The fact that in Jesus, I am living my life under the smiling countenance of God and that he is for me erupted in my heart. As my joy in that glorious status rose, fears sank, and I was free.

That is the glory we are made for, and only when we are satisfied with God's pleasure in us will we be free from the fear of displeasing everyone else. Only his approval will cure our hunger for glory. It can be ours by grace. The tragedy is that many will pass on it, discounting it and pining for the approval of mere men instead. When the apostle John tells us in John 12:42 that certain officials passed on Jesus because they "loved the glory that comes from men more than the glory that comes from God," John intends us to be shocked. In longing to be justified before men, they were forfeiting the ultimate justification. Longing to keep their standing before people, they forfeited their standing before the ultimate person. John was making sure we would know a glory hunger that is legitimate. There is a glory that we should long for and seek after, but it is not found from men. It's a glory that comes from God, a verdict he speaks over our lives. And it's a game-changer for the glory hungry.

Our Corruption Healed

As a child I was rather rambunctious. My hyperactivity often led to mischief and rebellion. My poor mom, in desperation, came up with the ingenious idea of a "be-nice shot." The be-nice shot was a miracle of modern medicine that would instantly turn a deviant child into a delightful one. Like all children, I hated shots, and the thought of going to the doctor to get a shot that could adjust my attitude was sufficient to adjust my attitude. However, one day I grew tired of my unruly self. Even as a young child I felt the inner struggle to be who I sensed I was meant to be. I was ready to be free from the struggle, so I went to my mom and requested that she take me to the doctor for the be-nice shot. Her cover was blown!

Although I would not have used these words, what I was feeling as a child was the passion to be free from the corruption of my fallen human nature. As one made in the image of God, Adam was created to reflect God. He was made to reflect his holiness and moral perfections, to mirror his attributes. Adam possessed unimaginable beauty, not just physically but also morally. He was radiant with virtue. But Adam failed, and his glory was diminished in the fall. As Adam's descendants, we are tainted by sin and fail to reflect the beauty God created us to possess and reflect. As those infected with Adam's moral corruption, ugly and inglorious things reside in our hearts and make their way into our lives: "evil thoughts, murder, adultery, sexual immorality, theft, false witness, slander," and these things "defile a person" (Matt. 15:18–19).

We feel this defilement. We often hang our heads in shame over it. We have skeletons in the closet that testify against us and make us out to be fools without sense or self-control. There are pictures of our past that expose the ugly flaws of our character. Our glory hunger can't handle this truth, so we hide those pictures and edit our profiles, trying to present ourselves as flawless people. Whether it was last year or last night, we have done things that we would rather forget and keep others from knowing about. We hate our defilement, and we want to be free from it—at least we do when we are sane.

One of the evidences that we desire to be truly good is the way we esteem virtue in others. I have noticed this especially during highly altruistic seasons such as Christmas. No one ever says, "I liked the old Ebenezer better." We prefer the new Ebenezer, who is gracious and generous. What we admire in others is a good indication of what we wish we saw in ourselves. When we are moved by the virtue of another, it is a reminder of the virtue we were made to possess and wish we possessed. Our aspiration toward virtue is the echo of Eden in our hearts. It is a longing to have the image of God, diminished and vandalized by sin, fully restored in us.

The gospel addresses our condemnation, assuring us that God does not condemn us for our corruption, because Jesus was condemned for us. Through his work, Jesus purchased the gift of the Holy Spirit, who now resides in us and is working to restore in us the glorious image of God. The old person we were before Jesus is progressively done away with as this new image is brought into clearer focus. Paul's words to the churches in Ephesus and Colossae affirm this to us:

> You have heard about him and were taught in him, as the truth is in Jesus, to put off your old self, which belongs to your former manner of life and is corrupt through deceitful desires, and to be renewed in the spirit of your minds, and to put on the new self, created after the likeness of God in true righteousness and holiness. (Eph. 4:21–24)

> Do not lie to one another, seeing that you have put off the old self with its practices and have put on the new self, which is being renewed in knowledge after the image of its creator. (Col. 3:9–10)

If we are in Jesus, we have the power to be done with the old self that belongs to our former manner of life, the old, inglorious self that was in Adam's image and suffered corruption. In Jesus, we are new and can experience a glorious renovation of our lives as we are renewed in the image of our Creator. The Holy Spirit is at work in us to make us more like Jesus, who is the very image and likeness of God (2 Cor. 4:4; Col. 1:15). Jesus is all that, deep down, we wish we were, and God will make us like him. As Christ is formed in us (Gal. 4:19), we are increasingly healed of our corruption and reflect the glorious image of God, bearing the fruit of love and all the virtues that go along with it. The outward glory so prized by the world will fade away, but inwardly we are renewed day by day (2 Cor. 4:16). As we behold Christ and exalt him as our Savior and the standard for our lives, we are changed from one degree of glory to the next (2 Cor. 3:18).

As we are changed, shameful behaviors lose their place in us. Those embarrassing outbursts of anger wane in their force and frequency. The hidden lusts that rage in our hearts are progressively subdued by love and self-control. The virtues we admire in others find increasing expression in our own lives. As God superintends this process, we find that we are not what we used to be. But also we are not what we are going to be. Similar to the current television home-makeover shows, our transformation is a process of renovation with a great reveal at the end. One day we will be made fully like Jesus, glorified before God, free from sin's humiliating presence in our lives, and we will no longer hang our heads in shame.

Our Greatness Restored

As one made in the image of God, Adam was the pinnacle of God's creative activity. He possessed a greatness that is hard for us on this side of the fall to imagine. Martin Luther explains that before Adam sinned,

> his intellect was the clearest, his memory was the best, and his will was the most straightforward—all in the most beautiful tranquility of mind, without any fear of death and without any anxiety. To these inner qualities came also the most beautiful and superb qualities of body and of all the limbs, qualities in which he surpassed all the remaining living creatures. I am fully

convinced that before Adam's sin, his eyes were so sharp and clear that they surpassed those of the lynx and eagle. He was stronger than the lions and the bears, whose strength is very great; and he handled them the way we handle puppies.[9]

That description sounds like a modern-day superhero, but it is what God intended for humanity. Adam was put on earth to rule, to exercise dominion over all the creatures that filled sky and sea and walked upon the ground (Gen. 1:26). He was to fill the earth with God's creative activity and exercise a commanding presence. Everything yielded to him as he was yielded to God. God gave this glory to Adam, and it was his only in relation to God and in submission to God. Yet Adam failed to exercise this dominion over the Serpent and instead yielded to it. He rebelled against God and gave up the rule that God had given him. He not only became corrupt in his nature, suffering guilt and condemnation, but also experienced the diminishing of God's designed greatness. He became weak, susceptible to the oppression of the elements and forced to do sweaty battle with the ground for daily bread. He eventually lost the battle and returned to the dust from which he came, suffering the ultimate shame.

As those who share in Adam's humanity, we were made to possess greatness. We were not meant to cower under the elements or the animals. We were not designed to be taunted by our weakening bodies. We were not meant to suffer sickness, injury, and certainly not death. We were meant to reign, not as tyrants who exploit the creation, but as God's vice-regents who reflect his character as we reign with him. That dominion has been frustrated, but we still have an ache for it. We want to win. We want to be on top. In the words of Tears for Fears, "Everybody wants to rule the world."[10] That glory hunger that manifests itself in our desire for greatness and control is a Genesis memory of what we were made for but what Adam lost. It is the residue of the image of God in us that gets twisted and can result in oppression and power trips, but it is also a hint of what we were made for and what God intends to restore to us in Jesus.

— In his life and ministry, Jesus demonstrated the dominion that God intended for humanity. He commanded the winds and waves, rebuked fever, overturned death, and crushed the head of the Serpent, as Adam couldn't. But that exercise of dominion was a foretaste of what is coming. For those who have sided with Jesus, the restoration of our glory culminates in Jesus's return to this world in glory and power. He will return as king and judge. "The kingdom of the world has become the kingdom of our God and of his Christ, and he shall reign forever and ever" (Rev. 11:15). And the promise to us is that "if we endure, we will also reign with him" (1 Tim. 2:12). We who fear the judgments of people will judge the world and angels at his coming (1 Cor. 6:2–3). We who want to rule our little corners of the globe will one day inherit the entire earth (Matt. 5:5). Jesus promises, "The one who conquers, I will grant him to sit with me on my throne, as I also conquered and sat down with my Father on his throne" (Rev. 3:21). Our glory hunger should lead us to Jesus, who has won for us an incomparable greatness we could never gain by our Sisyphean boulder pushing.

Jesus, the End of Our Glory Hunger

Our glory hunger can be a gift to lead us to the only one who can satiate it. Jesus is the end of our glory hunger. He restores to us the glory that Adam lost for us. This is why the Scriptures refer to Jesus as the second and final Adam:

> In Adam we glimpse the goodness and greatness that God intended for human creatures. Yet we only glimpse these, because Adam spoils them for all mankind, forfeiting them in the

first moments of the world. In Christ, we behold a second and greater Adam, the restorer of human goodness and greatness. What Adam squandered in a moment, the second Adam regains and bestows forever. As Paul writes in Romans 5:18, "As one trespass led to condemnation for all men, so one act of righteousness leads to justification and life for all men."[11]

Jesus is better than Adam in every way. Adam grasped for god-like status and plunged the world into sin and death. Jesus, "though he was in the form of God, did not count equality with God a thing to be grasped" (Phil. 2:6). Rather, he humbled himself by taking on flesh and, bearing our sin and condemnation, was plunged into an inglorious death so we could have our glory restored. That glory is God's affirming verdict over us and the renewal of our God-given capacity for greatness and dominion. In him we have the "very good" of God spoken over our lives as objects of the Father's pleasure. We are being renewed in his likeness, and we are destined for a greatness rivaled only by his. This is the glory we were made for.

4

Renouncing Narcissism

I recently read about a computer game called Kingdoms of Camelot in which players can gain "glory" by fighting other players. Your glory is always displayed, so you can see just how skillful you are and how you stack up against other players. You can show off your glory by making it viewable in the main gaming window, and when you hit glory milestones, special chat icons are displayed next to your name to indicate the glory you have secured. There is even a glory leaderboard. Every fourteen days, each player's glory resets to zero, and you must stay active if you want to stay atop the leaderboard. It sounds a lot like real life.

Life is a war for glory. Even those of us who have rested in Jesus to bring an end to our battle for glory still fight skirmishes in which we feel our reputations are at risk. We live on a battlefield where we strive to attain glory and put it on display. We measure ourselves against others to see how we are stacking up. Are we advancing in our careers fast enough? Is our romantic life lagging behind? Are our finances lagging behind? Are our gifted and talented children in all the right activities? Are we spiritual standouts? We become slaves to our image and the glory that comes from being extraordinary. With every victory the glory counter goes up, and with every failure and folly the glory counter is reset, and we strive to recapture that lost glory.

The gospel has the power to liberate us from that because Jesus won ultimate glory for us. In him we are given the unchanging status of justified and adopted children of God. We are fully known and fully loved. God's image is being restored in us, and we will one day "shine like the sun" (Matt. 13:43). What people say about us, what we say about ourselves, and what people do to us is trumped by what God has said about us and done for us in the gospel. But the skirmishes rage on, and we still fight for the glory that comes from men.

At the conclusion of C. S. Lewis's novel *Prince Caspian*, in The Chronicles of Narnia series, the valiant Reepicheep, a warrior mouse, has lost his tail in battle. In hope he comes before Aslan to plead for the restoration of his tail.

> "But what do you want with a tail?" asked Aslan. "Sir," said the Mouse, "I can eat and sleep and die for my King without one. But a tail is the honor and glory of a Mouse."
>
> "I have sometimes wondered, friend," said Aslan, "whether you do not think too much about your honor."[12]

I do not think we have to wonder but can assuredly know that we think too much about our honor and glory. When it comes to the issue of idolatry, pastors and theologians often refer to "near" and "far" idols, or "source" and "surface" idols. Far idols, or source idols, are the few deep idols that rule our hearts, those we seek to secure for our identity and joy. These far idols consist of control, power, approval, and comfort. Near idols, or surface idols, are those we use in an attempt to secure our far idols. For example, if our far idol is comfort, we might use a near idol such as food or pornography as an escape, a way to secure that comfort. If our far idol is power, we might use the near idol of money to give us a sense of power.

As we think through the issue of glory hunger and our desire for honor and recognition, we are dealing with the far idol of approval.

What we want more than anything is to have a sense of importance, significance, and worth, and it is possible that we treat Jesus and his gospel as a near idol to secure that far idol for us. Jesus's death and resurrection bestow on us glory and honor from the Father—absolutely. It is possible, though, that what we really want is not Jesus and God the Father but a sense of glory and honor that come to us from them in the gospel. Our hearts are so inclined to self that we can use the gospel of Jesus as an attempt to make ourselves indispensible to God.

The gospel says something wonderful about us, but it primarily says something wonderful about God. The cross is not primarily a shout-out to our worth but a shout-out to God's worth and righteousness, that he might be exalted as the "just and the justifier of the one who has faith in Jesus" (Rom. 3:26). The driving motivation of God's saving activity is the praise of his glory, not ours (Eph. 1:6, 12, 14). A legitimate glory hunger rooted in our need for God's love and acceptance can easily become warped and so remove God from the picture altogether and become a twisted and monstrous focus on self that uses the gospel to satisfy our obsession with our own significance and glory. Our legitimate glory hunger can easily get out of control and turn to narcissism.

Narcissus was a character in Greek mythology, a hunter well known for his beauty and vanity. One day his archrival led him to a pool where he stooped to drink. As he looked into the pool, he became transfixed by his reflection. Immobilized by his reflection but not knowing it was merely an image, he could not leave the reflection of his beauty, and he died beside the pool.

Narcissism lies at the core of our wrestling with glory hunger. While narcissism is a clinical issue, there is a functional narcissism that runs rampant in our culture. Narcissism is an excessive concern with and overinflated view of oneself, an inordinate self-love and preoccupation with one's own image and reputation. It is an egocentrism rooted in an exaggerated self-esteem that in reality is self-absorption.

Jean Twenge, in her work *The Narcissism Epidemic*, details this growing "I love me" culture. According to Twenge, a narcissist has an inflated opinion about himself and does whatever it takes to improve and promote his status, appearance, and importance. Twenge cites numerous examples and trends in our culture that expose the growth of narcissism.

For example, our culture is obsessed with the concept of self-love, and, frankly, loving yourself more than you love anyone else.

> As an NBC public service announcement puts it, "You may not realize it, but everyone is born with their one true love—themselves. If you like you, everyone else will, too."[13]

Twenge cites another writer, Diane Mastromarino, who wrote *The Girl's Guide to Loving Yourself: A Book about Falling in Love with the One Person Who Matters Most . . . You*: "Loving yourself means knowing how great you are and not letting any person, any place, or any thing ever get in the way of that."[14]

In our culture, real emotional health begins with an unabashed love affair with oneself. The message you are being sold is that you are great, and you matter more than anyone else.

Our Culture's Vanity

In his book *The Vertical Self: How Biblical Faith Can Help Us Discover Who We Are in an Age of Self-Obsession*, Mark Sayers shows us how our culture has lost its Christian identity. As a result, we are forced to forge an identity on our own, a horizontal self. We adopt worldly identities in an attempt to define ourselves. One of the key ingredients in the horizontal self is vanity.

As Sayers points out, being "hot" is now a cultural value. Whereas past generations esteemed virtues such as integrity, chivalry, responsibility, and respect, our culture today values the physical tangibles. This value is pushed and promoted by the countless images we see of airbrushed and Photoshopped supermodels on magazine covers and billboards. Good looks and a great body are the way to gain cultural approval and social capital, which is measured in the stares of others. According to Sayers, "In the media-drenched landscape in which we live, vanity is no longer a sin; it is a virtue."[15] In this atmosphere of celebrated vanity, many in our culture will spend whatever it takes to get the body and the look they feel they need to maintain their love of themselves and the attention and approval of others. Drastic increases in plastic surgery, breast augmentation, Botox, and hair removal reveal this obsession with appearance. Such things as teeth whitening are fairly new priorities. My dentist recently tried to convince me to get the newest offering in orthodontic technology to avoid the embarrassment of crooked teeth in my older years. Her pitch was made not on the basis of my health but on the fact that my unsightly bottom teeth will be more noticeable as my lower lip droops in old age. She seemed surprised by my lack of interest.

Our culture has become increasingly bold and unapologetic in its obsession with appearance. Twenge cites a *New York Times* article, "It's Botox for You, Dear Bridesmaids":

> Some brides are now asking their attendants to have cosmetic skin treatments. A Beverly Hills cosmetic surgeon says his business is up 40% since he began offering "Bridal Beauty Buffets" in 2006.[16]

In other words, "Don't mess up my special day with your poor complexion or unsightly figure. If you want to be in my party and in my pictures, near perfection is required."

Our Culture's Obsession with Celebrities and Our Quest for Fame

Our narcissistic culture has made celebrities into cultural icons and heroes, and celebrity status is now the holy grail. Becoming famous has become every child's dream and expectation. More than ever, people will do anything to be famous or even infamous. Herostratus was an arsonist who, in 356 BC, burned down the temple of Artemis in Ephesus, all with the hopes of becoming famous. His name became a term used to describe someone who commits a crime to make the news and be remembered. People want to be famous, or at least feel famous.

In her exposure of our culture's narcissism, Twenge references an Austin-based company, Celeb 4 A Day, founded with the intent of making customers feel as though they possess a measure of fame. The company provides clients with paparazzi to follow them around all night, taking pictures of them and their date or entourage, just like the stars. Clients get a fake celebrity magazine at the end of the evening with their picture on the front cover. The surprising thing is that people pay three thousand dollars for this treatment. The service has become so popular that it has spread into Los Angeles and New York City. As Twenge notes, Counting Crows summed it up best in their song "Mr. Jones and Me": "When I look at the television I want to see me staring right back at me; we all want to be big stars."[17] Sadly, even big stars can't get enough stardom. The British rock star Amy Winehouse tragically overdosed and died watching YouTube videos of her performances. The quest for celebrity status might find expression in different ways in different fields or domains, but there is a growing obsession with personal clout.

Our Constant Broadcasting of Ourselves for Fame

Speaking of clout, individuals create personal clout through social media. Social media is not bad, but it can be used badly. The Internet is a venue for self-promotion. YouTube enables people to broadcast themselves and gain a measure of celebrity status, even if only among their own social tribes. Other social media sites such as Facebook and Twitter are public arenas where people post anything to get fans and admirers, even at the cost of personal dignity or the dignity of someone else. Social media allows us to present a digitally edited version of our lives that we can present to others, hiding what we want to hide and highlighting what we want to highlight. Mark Sayers writes,

> Just think of the millions of hours people across the world now spend cultivating their online identities on sites such as Facebook, Twitter, and MySpace, tweaking the images and identities they wish to broadcast to the world. Never before has humanity spent such an inordinate amount of time making ourselves look good. Today we do not even blink at such narcissism; it has become a lynchpin of youth culture.[18]

Such a rush comes from this narcissistic promotion of self that one study recently concluded that people get as much pleasure from tweeting about themselves as they do from eating or having sex. One recently failed addition to the online narcissism scene was a company called Fame. The purpose of their site was to give its users the opportunity to have one million Twitter followers for a day. Mashable.com describes the company's service:

> When users authorize Fame to access their Twitter accounts, they're entered into a daily drawing. The winner is automatically followed by all of the other entrants. At the end of the day, that person is automatically unfollowed by everyone, and a new person is selected.[19]

We are so concerned with our social clout that it can now be calculated. Klout.com will measure your presence, popularity, and influence on the Internet. The website says,

We measure your influence based on your ability to drive action in social networks. We process this data on a daily basis to give you an updated Klout Score each morning.

Each day Klout.com traces how many retweets and mentions you get on Twitter and how many comments, wall posts, and likes you get on Facebook, in addition to other social media activity. And each morning you can begin your day knowing how significant you really are. Has a generation ever been so concerned with its own glory?

The Crushing Consequences of Narcissism

There is a temptation to say, "So what if our culture is narcissistic!" But there are some tragic and destructive consequences to functional narcissism. Proverbs warns us, "It is not good to eat much honey, nor is it glorious to seek one's own glory" (Prov. 25:27). In other words, just as you can get sick eating too much honey, you can get sick on an appetite for personal glory. Eugene Peterson, in his book *Where Your Treasure Is: Psalms That Summon You from Self to Community*, writes, "Centering life in the insatiable demands of the ego is the sure path to doom."[20] We don't have to read too far in the biblical narrative to see this. The great temptation with which Satan deceived Adam and Eve was to become their own gods, putting themselves at the center—what some have called the "de-godding" of God and the deification of self. When they bit on that temptation, sin and death entered this world, and the cosmos become chaos.

Narcissistic people rarely have deep friendships and usually don't really desire them. They have fans but not friends. They have the admiration of others but not intimacy. They want to surround themselves with those who will approve and affirm them and assure them that they are okay but not with true friends who will lovingly wound them with the truth. They don't typically give in relationships; they tend to take. Narcissists tend to use others to build up themselves but do not invest or give in relationships. So relationships for narcissists, whether personal or professional, have a short shelf life. Narcissism also induces anxiety. Constantly comparing oneself with others and feeling the pressure of keeping up are great burdens.

A narcissistic glory hunger is destructive primarily because it means that one has taken a life direction that is opposite to reality. If we are going to truly flourish as human beings, we can't create an alternate reality, a little world with ourselves at the center. That is what lies at the root of illegitimate glory hunger—an inordinate concern with and attentiveness to oneself. A world with everything orbiting around us will crumble, because it is not real. We are not God and cannot shoulder the burden of being God. It is like that image of the little kitten looking in a mirror and seeing a lion. The caption reads, "What matters most is how you see yourself." There is some truth to this. In particular, how we see ourselves before God does impact how we live in God's world. But we also know that it is not all true, and the cat will soon discover that, should it face off with a large, ferocious dog.

What matters most is what is real. If we are going to be whole and flourish, we must move in the direction of ultimate reality, which means we need to center our lives on the right thing. *We must glorify most what is most glorious. We must love most what is most lovely. We must value supremely what is supremely valuable.* The only way out of thinking too much about our glory, loveliness, and value is to be captured by a vision of the glorious, lovely, supremely valuable God. A vision of God's greatness and a zeal for his clout and fame are the only things that will displace a zeal for personal clout and fame. It is this passion we see most fully in Jesus.

If anyone could have rightfully been a narcissist, it was Jesus.

He was God in the flesh. He was sinless and never lost an argument. But he came not to be served but to serve and give his life as a ransom for many (Matt. 20:28). Jesus was not consumed with a passion for his glory.

In John 12, before we hear the indictment on those who believed in Jesus but refused to confess him openly because they wanted the glory that comes from men, John records an audible conversation Jesus had with the Father:

> Now is my soul troubled. And what shall I say? "Father, save me from this hour"? But for this purpose I have come to this hour. Father, glorify your name." Then a voice came from heaven: "I have glorified it, and I will glorify it again." (John 12:27–28)

On the brink of Jesus's most horrific hour, his focus was on the Father's name being glorified. His soul was deeply troubled. The word translated "troubled" carries the connotation of disturbed, frightened, even terrified. Jesus was unsettled and fearful over what he was about to face. He would be betrayed by a friend, denied by another, abandoned by the rest. He would be falsely accused of blaspheming his Father, whom he perfectly loved. He would be mocked, beaten, scourged, humiliated, and brutally crucified. The physical agonies would pale in comparison to the emotional and spiritual anguish he would undergo. He was to bear all the sins of those who would believe in him and take on the full fury of the wrath of God in their place. He would feel the crushing alienation of being forsaken by the Father, with whom he had lived in unbroken fellowship. Could anything be more terrifying? For Jesus, the answer was yes. The prospect of escaping that hour and failing to bring the Father glory and honor through full obedience was a more terrifying alternative.

Jesus's passion was to glorify the Father's name. The involuntary, spontaneous eruption of his heart in this soul-disturbing moment was, "Father, glorify your name." That is why Jesus came. The cross is primarily about God's glory. It is about God's holiness and righteousness and justice being upheld and vindicated in the forgiveness of sinners, that he might be "just and the one who justifies the ungodly" (Rom. 3:26). The cross was Jesus's finest hour because it was the hour when he preserved the Father's glory and put it on display, which was the greatest longing of Jesus's heart. Throughout John's Gospel, we see that Jesus's driving desire was to honor the Father:

> If anyone's will is to do God's will, he will know whether the teaching is from God or whether I am speaking on my own authority. The one who speaks on his own authority seeks his own glory; but the one who seeks the glory of him who sent him is true, and in him there is no falsehood. (John 7:17–19)

Jesus did not live for his own agenda, seeking his own glory. He was fully yielded to the authority of his Father. Later Jesus says, "I do not seek my own glory" (John 8:50). It was not in his heart to compete with the Father for glory. He was here to do what the Father sent him to do. His glory and honor would be found in glorifying the Father.

> I glorified you on earth, having accomplished the work that you gave me to do. And now, Father, glorify me in your own presence with the glory that I had with you before the world existed. (John 17:4–5)

Jesus was fixed in his passion for the Father's glory. His whole life, from incarnation to exaltation, was about glorifying the Father. In the hour of his crucifixion, Jesus would indeed be glorified (John 12:23). He would be glorified as the fully obedient, suffering servant. He would have his preincarnate glory restored to him. The Father would make sure of that.

The Father raised him and exalted him and bestowed upon him the highest name. He has been glorified in heaven, seated at the right hand of the Father with the glory he had before his incarnation, and he is to be worshiped, exalted, and honored above all things. But Jesus did not seek this glory from the world. He sought glory from the Father, who bestowed it upon him, as he sought glory for the Father. What a contrast to our first parents and to our impulse as their descendants. Adam and Eve sought glory apart from the Father by disobeying the Father, and it resulted in their shame and humiliation. Jesus sought glory from the Father by fully submitting to the Father, and it resulted ultimately in his exaltation and honor.

In a world consumed with personal glory, Jesus shows us the way to life. His invitation is to lose our life—to renounce our obsessive concern with ourselves and make the glory of God our consuming desire. Life and freedom are found not in satisfying the insatiable demands of our ego but in centering our lives on something entirely outside of ourselves, bigger than ourselves. When we, like Jesus, love most what is most lovely, and value supremely what is supremely valuable, and glorify most what is most glorious, we will begin to experience freedom from the crippling concern of glorifying ourselves. We will be delivered from our obsession to be loved and honored when we are consumed with a greater desire—for the Father to be loved and honored. The ruling desire of our hearts must be to love the Father like Jesus loved the Father; to be less preoccupied with ourselves and more preoccupied with God.

5

Ordering Glory

I don't have any scientific data to back this up other than my own experimentation with my kids, but ask a small child who has not been schooled in basic money matters to choose between a nickel and dime, and most of the time that child will choose the nickel. Though the dime has more value, the size of the nickel fools them every time.

We are constantly being tested on our ability to choose the greatest value. There is a daily battle going on for the capture of our heart. The first commandment teaches us that. When God commands us to have no other gods before him, he is letting us know that our hearts will be tempted to worship something less valuable than the rightful object of worship. The greatest temptation we face is to choose the nickel of our glory over the infinite value of the Father's. The biggest danger to our lives is pride, the worship of self, and the excessive concern for our renown.

Jesus was free from this. In Jesus we see the perfect picture of one who was absolutely resolute about seeking glory for the Father only and from the Father only. This is what he came to do for us and in us. Jesus came to win glory for us, securing a verdict and status over us with the Father that can satisfy our every pang of glory hunger. Having glory that comes from the ultimate person, we are set free from needing glory from anyone else. And once we know the glorious Father, Jesus works in us to want glory for the Father.

He is working in us to be less preoccupied with ourselves and more preoccupied with God, which is the key to our happiness. Until we love most what is most lovely, and glorify most what is most glorious, and value supremely what is supremely valuable, we will not be living in step with reality, and we will sabotage our life.

In his book *Reordered Love, Reordered Lives*, David Naugle instructs us from Augustine on the importance of getting our loves in the right order so that God might be properly honored and that we might be truly happy and fulfilled:

> According to Augustine, "There is a scale of value stretching from earthly to heavenly realities, from the visible to the invisible; and the inequality between these goods makes possible the existence of them all." God is one thing, angels are another, as are people, terriers, red oaks, squash, rocks, and dirt. Each item fits in God's overall scheme of creation. The nature of things in the hierarchy is unchangeable, and so is the kind of satisfaction it can provide when we are related to it through love. Because of these actual differences in things, the outcome of loving each actual thing will be different. There is a divinely designed fit between our needs, the character of the things that can satisfy them, and the way we should love them in order to be satisfied. Even though each thing God made is good, delightful, legitimate, and a source of satisfaction as an object of our love, we "must not expect more from it than its unique nature can provide." We must give love and praise to things apportioned to their worth.[21]

The joy you get from loving an object is directly proportional to the glory of that object. The greater the glory of the object, the greater the joy you get from loving it. Each thing in the universe provides a level of joy and satisfaction that is bound up in its essential nature. It's one thing to gaze at a crack in the sidewalk, but your heart and soul tell you it's another thing to stand on the edge of the Grand Canyon.

I have a friend whose wife loves living in the country. One day she called my friend and said, "John, I'm in the garden, smelling a handful of dirt, and I love it. Thank you for letting us live in the country." But I am certain that the joy she experienced from smelling her newborn baby far surpassed the joy that came from smelling dirt. The essential nature of a baby and its divine design is such that loving that baby provides more joy than a handful of dirt ever could.

One evidence of our fallen nature is that our affections tend to be disproportionate to the object loved. We know something is wrong with our heart when we prefer intrinsically lesser objects over greater ones, when the dirt is more joyful than the baby. We see this in the alcoholic who would prefer to have one more drink rather than leave the pub to attend his kid's birthday party. And we see it in anyone who is more attentive to self than to God.

As we follow the hierarchy of realities, we find at the top, uncontested and unrivaled, the glorious and incomparable God. If we want to be happy, we must order our loves rightly by loving him above all things. As Naugle put it, "We must give love and praise to things apportioned to their worth." We must ascribe the most worth to what is most worthy. If we give something more love and praise than it is worthy of, then we are expecting from it what "its unique nature cannot provide," and we will be devastated. The application of this truth is far-reaching. How many parents seek too much soul satisfaction from their children and end up crushing them under the unreasonable expectations of that disordered love? The same could be said for any relationship—we ruin the very joy God intends for us to find in it when we expect a measure of joy that the essential nature of the relationship cannot provide.

This is especially relevant to the issue of our glory hunger. When our glory and reputation and name are of greater concern to us than God's, we are loving ourselves more than God. We are centering our joy on ourselves. It's no wonder that we end up miserable, unable to bear up under the rank and responsibilities of being God. We are pathetic at being God. We are not built to bear the weight of being worshiped, by ourselves or by anyone else. It corrupts and crushes us. The life and joy that God intends for us is found only in a rightly ordered love for God and a rightly ordered love of self. This is what the gospel is designed to do—free us from the worship of self and bring us into the joy of worshiping God. The great aim of the gospel is not to redefine us to feel wonderful about ourselves but to reorient us to God so that we lose our attentiveness to self altogether and give our attention to the most worthy object. This is key to our joy and freedom. I believe this is what Paul is driving at in Romans 15:

> I tell you that Christ became a servant to the circumcised to show God's truthfulness, in order to confirm the promises given to the patriarchs, and in order that the Gentiles might glorify God for his mercy. (vv. 8–9)

Christ came so that God might be seen as one who keeps his promises. He promised Israel a Messiah, a servant; and in the incarnation, life, death, and resurrection of Jesus, God fulfilled his promises. And God included the Gentiles in this salvation as well, that he might be known and worshiped by all nations as a merciful God. In other words, the cross is not intended to make us turn our gaze inward, marveling at ourselves as objects of mercy, but to make us turn our gaze upward and marvel at the merciful, promise-keeping God. As we read the Scriptures, we see that God is at work through redemptive history, exalting himself so that his people might be brought into the glad enjoyment of his beauty, power, grace, wisdom, and worth, all the while losing our infatuation with our own worth. We must be vigilant to reorder our loves and seek to love and glorify the triune God above all things.

The Character and Nature of God

The first key to reordering our loves is to seriously contemplate the nature and character of God. The Psalms are a wonderful help for doing just that. In the words of Eugene Peterson, they "summon us away from ourselves" because they give us such a massive vision of God.[22] I have found Psalm 145 immensely helpful in thinking proper thoughts about God and about myself and helping me to reorder my loves. The psalm speaks of God's greatness, his grace, and his dominion and leaves us in jaw-dropping wonder, forgetting ourselves, ready to join the psalmist in extolling and blessing God forever:

> I will extol you, my God and King,
>> and bless your name forever and ever.
> Every day I will bless you
>> and praise your name forever and ever.
> Great is the LORD, and greatly to be praised,
>> and his greatness is unsearchable.
> One generation shall commend your works to another,
>> and shall declare your mighty acts.
> On the glorious splendor of your majesty,
>> and on your wondrous works, I will meditate.
> They shall speak of the might of your awesome deeds,
>> and I will declare your greatness.
> They shall pour forth the fame of your abundant goodness
>> and shall sing aloud of your righteousness. (vv. 1–7)

We learn from the outset of the psalm that God is great and is to be praised with fervency and passion, with the fullness of our being. God's greatness is unsearchable (v. 3). His power is beyond full comprehension and exceeds our capacity for understanding. We can't fathom all that God is capable of. Job testified to this when he said, "Behold, these are but the outskirts of his ways, and how small a whisper do we hear of him! But the thunder of his power who can understand?" (Job 26:14). When Job speaks of the outskirts of God's ways, he is speaking of the fringes, the extremities, the mere edge, or a minute part of God's power and capabilities. There is cosmos-shaking thunder with God, but all we have heard is the whisper. The whisper has been awe-inspiring, but we could not handle the thunder. We are blown away by the bottle rocket–sized expressions of God's power; we could not handle the Space Shuttle–sized. Stephen Charnock, the Puritan writer, tells us that when we consider all the works of God in creation and in redemptive history,

> these are but little crumbs and fragments of that Infinite Power, which is, in his nature, like a drop in comparison of the mighty ocean; a hiss or whisper in comparison with a mighty voice of thunder.[23]

In other words, God is infinitely more capable of displays of power, wisdom, beauty, terror, and wonder than what we see in the most breathtaking and humbling of his displays. Think of a time when you have been stunned by a storm or a sunset, or a vista or an ocean, or a newborn—these are but the outskirts, the mere edges, the small fragments of what God is capable of. These things are the low-volume works of God. When we say that God is capable of more, it is not like the one-notch-louder "11" setting in *Spinal Tap*. There is infinitely more volume that this world cannot contain and we cannot handle.

The biblical writers grasp for every image they can find to drive home the greatness and power and splendor of God's majesty. In

Isaiah 40 the prophet tells us that God is so great that he measures all the waters of the world in the palm of his hand and measures the heavens with the span of his hand. I can barely palm a basketball. This great God can collect all the dust of the earth in a basket—the Sahara, the Arabian Desert, and every other desert plain and beach swept up. He can weigh the mountains on a scale—Everest, the Himalayas, and the Rockies all weighed in ounces. All the nations, Isaiah tells us, are like a drop of water from a bucket—insignificant and posing no threat to a sovereign God. And if every ruler, king, prince, or pope were to rally against this God, he would blow on them, and they would wither like grass in a fire. We read in Isaiah 40, "To whom then will you liken God?" (v. 18), and "To whom then will you compare me?" (v. 25). He is in a class all by himself. No one can stand toe-to-toe or eye-to-eye with him. He is the great and incomparable God. And if he does not hold the highest place in our hearts, trumping our own name, we ruin ourselves. He is great and greatly to be praised.

Psalm 145 continues:

> The LORD is gracious and merciful,
>> slow to anger and abounding in steadfast love.
> The LORD is good to all,
>> and his mercy is over all that he has made.
> All your works shall give thanks to you, O LORD,
>> and all your saints shall bless you!
> They shall speak of the glory of your kingdom
>> and tell of your power,
> to make known to the children of man your mighty deeds,
>> and the glorious splendor of your kingdom.
> Your kingdom is an everlasting kingdom,
>> and your dominion endures throughout all generations.
> [The LORD is faithful in all his words
>> and kind in all his works.]

The LORD upholds all who are falling
    and raises up all who are bowed down.
The eyes of all look to you,
    and you give them their food in due season.
You open your hand;
    you satisfy the desire of every living thing.
The LORD is righteous in all his ways
    and kind in all his works.
The LORD is near to all who call on him,
    to all who call on him in truth.
He fulfills the desire of those who fear him;
    he also hears their cry and saves them.
The LORD preserves all who love him,
    but all the wicked he will destroy.
My mouth will speak the praise of the LORD,
    and let all flesh bless his holy name forever and ever.
      (vv. 8–21)

We also learn from Psalm 145 that God is abundant in goodness. It is terrifying to think that God would be great but not good. But our God is great and always possesses a surplus of goodness. He never reaches the end of his kindness. This great God is good to all, and his mercy is over all, which is God's general goodness or *common grace* (vv. 9, 15–17). He is generous and kind and merciful to everyone. He generously opens his hand and meets the needs of every living thing. Jesus taught us that God causes the rain to fall on the just and the unjust. Even to his enemies God is kind, giving life and blood and breath and beauty and joys.

But there is also a saving grace, a particular goodness for which the psalmist extols God (v. 8). God is gracious, slow to anger, and abounding in steadfast love. This is the same language God used when he revealed himself to Moses in Exodus 34:6 as the God who keeps covenant with his chosen people:

The Lord descended in the cloud and stood with him there, and proclaimed the name of the Lord. The Lord passed before him and proclaimed, "The Lord, the Lord, a God merciful and gracious, slow to anger, and abounding in steadfast love and faithfulness, keeping steadfast love for thousands, forgiving iniquity and transgression and sin, but who will by no means clear the guilty, visiting the iniquity of the fathers on the children and the children's children, to the third and the fourth generation." (Ex. 34:5–7)

That is the posture God takes toward his covenant people. He is gracious, saving, and loving. Psalm 145:18–20 highlights this. He is near to those who call on him in truth. He fulfills the desires of those who fear him. In other words, those who value him supremely and humbly acknowledge his right to their lives experience his nearness and his promise to do good to them forever. He hears their cry and saves, delivers, and rescues them. This is the great and gracious God who alone deserves the highest rank in our life.

I find Psalm 145 strikingly relevant to the issue of our glory hunger. Our culture desires to possess greatness or at least to be near it. Have you ever been around a name dropper? If we can't possess greatness ourselves, we at least want to be associated with those we perceive to have it and are superior to us. Psalm 145 challenges that desire and at the same time fulfills it. It calls us to give up on our own greatness because there is one whose greatness eclipses ours. But it is a greatness that we can be near. We can be on a first-name basis with God. The I AM is the only name we will ever have to drop. It is here that our quest for greatness ends. There is an incomparably great one who is also gracious and welcomes us and will bring us near to him and show us his steadfast love, forever. He does so, not that we can feel special but so that we can forget about ourselves altogether, having our attention and affection seized by something greater.

Psalm 145 also gives us a vision of the dominion of God. He is the king over all the earth. His dominion has no end. The Scriptures tell us that God is in the heavens, and he does all he pleases (Ps. 115:3). But his rule is not oppressive. Psalm 145 tells us that God's dominion, his rule, is eternal (everlasting and enduring throughout all generations), but it is also tender. He upholds those who are falling and raises up all who are bowed down. For those who delight in his rule, God's reign is not one that crushes but one that restores; not one that tears down but one that lifts up. But the psalmist is clear: you can love, trust, honor, and call upon this eternal king, or you can rebel against him. You can keep yourself at the center and refuse to have him as your God, but then his dominion will be a crushing one. This king is tender, but he is not a trifle; he is not to be taken lightly.

So we see that God is great, he is gracious, and he has all authority and dominion. Psalm 145 celebrates him as such. This song is radically different from the songs our culture produces that unabashedly celebrate self. Psalm 145 orients us away from self, into a reflection and meditation and celebration of the greatness, grace, and life-giving dominion of God. Our culture needs the psalms to help us reorder our attention and affections. Psalms like this one help us worship our way out of our narcissism and glory hunger, putting our attention on what is truly glorious and satisfying us with that glory.

I find myself at times envying the psalm writers for their clear vision of God. But, actually, we are the envy of the psalmist. Jesus told his disciples:

> Blessed are your eyes, for they see, and your ears, for they hear. For truly, I say to you, many prophets and righteous people longed to see what you see, and did not see it, and to hear what you hear, and did not hear it. (Matt. 13:16–17)

We know and have seen something the author of Psalm 145 did not. He longed to see what we have seen and hear what we have heard. We have seen the greatness and grace and dominion of God in living color. God the Son has come in the flesh. He is the visible image of the invisible God (Col. 1:15). He has come to fully reveal, or exegete, the Father to us (John 1:18).

In chapters 4 and 5 of Mark's Gospel we see the greatness, grace, and dominion of God in the person of Christ. Mark 4 ends with Jesus and his disciples in a boat crossing the Sea of Galilee. This large body of water is surrounded by large hills, and often the wind violently stirs up the sea. On this particular occasion, the wind has created a storm that even those seasoned fisherman could not manage. As they struggle against the wind and waves, Jesus lies sleeping. He is tired, because he is fully man, but he is about to do something that only God can do. His disciples wake him and ask him one of the most ironic questions ever asked in Scripture: "Teacher, do you not care that we are perishing?" (v. 38). Yes, he does care, and he will show them that fully at the cross, when the tempest of God's wrath against us breaks upon him. But in this moment he will show his disciples in a practical way that he possesses the power to save the perishing. He wakes, rises, and, with a word, he calms a raging sea. As the winds die and the water becomes still like glass, the disciples discover a new fear, an overwhelming awe at the greatness of God encased in human flesh standing in their boat.

As they land on the other side of the sea, Jesus encounters a demon-possessed man who is out of his mind, unclothed, and inflicting injury upon himself. He has been living in isolation among tombs. He is unclean, untouchable, and bound by the dominion of Satan. Everyone has given up on him, and he has had no hope for a better existence. But in a remarkable act of grace and power, Jesus exercises the dominion of God, casts out the demons, and sets up his kingdom in the heart of this one who had been ruled by darkness. The scene ends with the man clothed, unbound, in his right mind, and restored. Jesus gave him back his liberty and his life.

We see the power and grace of God in Christ as he heals a woman who for twelve years has suffered from an incurable disease that has rendered her unclean. Her condition has led her into a life of loneliness as a social and religious outcast. Even though the crowds flinch at her nearness, in a moment of bold desperation she works her way through a mob of people, reaches out her hand, and touches the *fringes*, the outer edges, of Jesus's robe. At once, power goes out from Jesus, and she is healed. Having been found out, she kneels before Jesus and confesses to the contaminating touch. But he is not contaminated, nor does he hold her in contempt. He speaks to her affectionately, blessing her with peace and calling her "daughter." I wonder how long it had been since anyone had spoken to her with such affection.

Mark 5 ends with Jesus entering a tearful room of a little twelve-year-old girl who has just died. As a daddy, it is hard to fathom losing one of my little girls. The presence of pain and grief in that room had to have been thick. But the presence of Jesus was thicker. He tenderly and graciously touches the corpse and speaks to the girl, "Little girl, I say to you, arise" (v. 41). Jesus brings her back from the dead and gives her to her mother and father.

In his healings we see that his greatness, power, and dominion are not oppressive but tender. The prophecy was fulfilled in him: "A bruised reed he will not break, and a faintly burning wick he will not snuff out" (Isa. 42:3). Jesus upheld those who were falling and raised up those who were bowed down, and these are but the fringes of his ways.

The revelation of God in Christ reaches its zenith when this great one humbled himself in grace and love and died in our place so that we could be forgiven and restored to the Father. He died so that we might be forgiven of our self-worship. He was crushed and snuffed out so we would not have to be. The Father raised him from the dead and bestowed upon him the name that is above every name and granted to him all rule, power, authority, and dominion.

Now the invitation of this great and gracious king is that we would die to ourselves, *unself* our lives, and center on him so that we might really live. Come and trust the one who is most trustworthy; love most the one who is most lovely. Glorify most the one who is most glorious. Value supremely the one who is supremely valuable. Move in the direction of reality instead of constructing your own reality that will crumble in the end. Our joy depends upon this reordering of our loves. God does not satisfy us by giving us great thoughts about ourselves but by giving to us something truly great—himself, in the person of his Son.

When the glory and renown of God revealed in creation and in his Son are the delight of our hearts, and when the ruling desire of our hearts is for his fame and honor to increase in all the earth, the desire for our own glory and fame is drowned out. Our narcissistic glory hunger is decimated in a vision of God's uncontested glory.

So it is imperative that we meditate on the gospel of God and on the glory of God. In doing so, our hearts will rejoice and rest in God for his unearned love and acceptance, and our hearts will surrender the war against God for glory that belongs only to him. That surrender is not a loss but a victory; it is not a sorrow but a joy. As we see and delight in the glory of God in Christ, we begin to rightly order our affections. It is what Thomas Chalmers so famously called "the expulsive power of a new affection."

We have experienced this in different arenas of our lives. For example, many students do not wind up majoring in the subject they entered the university to study. After taking a course or two in another field, they shifted their interest; they found the other field to be more compelling and one that resonated with how they have been hardwired. Maybe they had a professor whose passion was contagious and lit up their heart over the subject. Their interest in business was expelled by their fascination with marine biology, or their newly discovered passion for education overruled their original interest in finance.

Spiritually, we are born majoring on ourselves. We are fixated on our name, honor, and glory. But when God opens our eyes to the beauty, supremacy, and glory of his Son in his life, death, resurrection, and exaltation, our interest shifts, and our major changes. Our hearts get lit up by a vision of the glory of God in Christ, and we find it to be more compelling than our own. Our narcissism is obliterated by a new affection. This is why the psalmist could cry out,

> Not to us, O Lord, not to us, but to your name give glory,
> for the sake of your steadfast love and your faithfulness!
> Why should the nations say,
> "Where is their God?"
> Our God is in the heavens;
> he does all that he pleases. (Ps. 115:1–3)

As the psalmist reflects on the sovereignty and supremacy of God and recounts the steadfast love and faithfulness of God, he renounces himself as the object of worship. He refuses glory for his own name and longs for glory to be given to God. We have to worship our way out of our narcissistic glory hunger. Calvin's *Institutes* begins with this very idea:

> Men are never duly touched and impressed with a conviction of their insignificance, until they have contrasted themselves with the majesty of God.[24]

When our hearts are brought low and lit up over the greatness and grace of God, now fully seen in Christ, we cease to major on ourselves, adamantly rejecting self-glory and redirecting the attention and acclaim where it is properly due.

When my annual school yearbook came out, I would flip to the index, find my name, and look for all the pages where my picture was. Sometimes it was a good year, and my picture was on several pages. Other years I languished in obscurity, appearing only on the page where my personal mug shot had been placed. I remember how happy I was to see my picture on multiple pages and also how ripped off I felt for buying the yearbook and finding very few pictures of myself. But real life is not like a yearbook. God will not make us happy by filling up our world with pictures of ourselves so that we can feel important; that is narcissism. I've realized that God will make me happy by filling up my world with pictures of him so that I lose my preoccupation with myself and feel the wonder and awe for which I am really hungry. The only way to win in this life is to lose the war for glory, to choose what is truly valuable, and to surrender to God the highest place in our hearts.

6

Don't Look at Me!

I'm always entertained when fans at sporting events see themselves on the Jumbotron. They are sitting calmly in conversation until someone shows them they are on the screen, and then they just snap. There is a brief look of panic followed by frantic waving or pose striking. Some have waited for this opportunity and know exactly what to do for their big-screen debut. It is crazy how normal folks who, moments earlier were sitting down enjoying a baseball game, will engage in crazy antics for the cameraman during the seventh inning stretch, hoping for a few seconds of fame.

With the ubiquity of smartphones, many of us carry around our own little Jumbotron in our purses or pockets. This is the age of the selfie. People love to see themselves and promote their image for the world to see. There was even a national selfie portrait gallery on display in October of 2013 at London's Moving Image Contemporary Art Fair. The selfie is the modern-day version of the self-portrait, except now you don't have to be a legitimate artist to create one, just a narcissist with a smartphone. This "look at me" mania was put on display at the 2013 College World Series when two young ladies rushed out on the field to take a selfie, later posting a video of themselves being tackled by security and earning Internet fame in the process. I guess it never occurred to the young ladies that the thousands of people who dropped good money to watch skilled athletes compete for a national championship were not actually there to see them. Something significant was taking place on that field, but in their minds the field was their stage and this was their time.

I'm sure the two selfie-snappers are nice gals, but in that moment, their narcissism got the best of them. It gets the best of all of us. We are prone to thinking we are the point. We can be like a batboy at the World Series who thinks the crowd is there to watch him retrieve bats and misses the fact that the great game is bigger than him and his part in it.[25] No baseball almanac keeps stats on batboys. Batboys are not the point of baseball, and we are not the point of life.

Like our first parents who grasped to be like God, we have an innate tendency to try to compete with God. While all the hosts of heaven never cease giving him praise, we maneuver for the spotlight. We don't literally expect people to bow down to us or compose songs about us, but we are motivated by the thrill of being praised, recognized, or remembered. We can be like glory scrapbookers— thrilled when we see our name in print, clipping out and holding on to any mention that might make us feel important.

The Bible takes a pastoral tone when it encourages us to worship our way out of our narcissistic glory hunger. But it also takes a prophetic tone, offering hard words that snap us back into reality by forcing us to contemplate the end of everything that would compete with God for glory. God has promised a bleak and disappointing end to those who value their glory above his own. God speaks in devastating language in the Scriptures when he addresses the glory hungry who seek to establish their importance, impressiveness, and notoriety. In God's estimate, to seek your own glory is to seek against his. He is not amused by our running out into the cosmos snapping selfies, yelling, "Look at me!" while the whole earth is full of his glory. This is God's world, and our lives are lived before him as either the humble who delight in his name or the haughty who delight in our name. A day is coming when God alone will be exalted and when he will irrevocably reveal the transience of every glory raised up against his own. All lights that have generated their own brightness will be washed out by the brilliance of his glorious light forever.

That is a major theme of the prophet Isaiah, whose ministry began with a vision of the glory of God in the temple (Isa. 6:1–8). He saw the Lord high and exalted, enthroned as the sovereign king. With wide eyes, weak knees, and devastated pride, Isaiah took in the terror of a holy God, whose glory was so robust that the whole earth could not contain it. Isaiah was humbled to the point of crying out, "Woe is me! For I am lost; for I am a man of unclean lips, and I dwell in the midst of a people of unclean lips; for my eyes have seen the King, the Lord of hosts!" (v. 5). In the light of God's glory, he was stripped of his own. Few could hold their own against Isaiah, but up against God, Isaiah is leveled. Compared to God, Isaiah's glory and righteousness are revealed as infinitely inadequate. By the grace of God, he is cleansed from his sin and commissioned to God's service. This experience made him the ideal spokesman to God's people and those of the surrounding nations who had exalted themselves above God. Throughout his prophecy, in devastating fashion, Isaiah confronts the glory hungry of his day with a dose of reality about how the universe works:

> The haughty looks of man shall be brought low,
>   and the lofty pride of men shall be humbled,
>   and the Lord alone will be exalted in that day.
>
> For the Lord of hosts has a day
>   against all that is proud and lofty,
>   against all that is lifted up—and it shall be brought low; . . .

> And the haughtiness of man shall be humbled,
> > and the lofty pride of men shall be brought low,
> > and the LORD alone will be exalted in that day. (Isa.
> > 2:11–12, 17)

A day is coming when the glory of God will triumph over the glory of men. In this coming day of the Lord, God will establish his kingdom upon the earth in its fullness. Kings and kingdoms will be brought to naught. But the day of the Lord has several dress rehearsals, as God presently deals a decisive, humiliating blow to prideful, God-belittling nations. Isaiah unapologetically denounces the kings of his day and their kingdoms as momentary and their glory as passing. Isaiah warns Babylon that though they are "the glory of kingdoms, the splendor and pomp of the Chaldeans," they will be brought low, devastated and overthrown like Sodom and Gomorrah (13:19). "The glory of Moab will be brought into contempt" (16:14). And Isaiah informs Tyre and Sidon that the Lord has purposed "to defile the pompous pride of all glory, to dishonor all the honored of the earth" (23:9). In the end, "the glory of the LORD will be revealed, and all flesh shall see it together" (40:5). God makes clear through his prophet that he will not give his glory to any other (42:8; 48:11). In the end, the Lord will share the stage with no one.

It's tempting to read such sections of Scripture and think of God as a petty, pouting glory hog who can't stand the thought of someone else getting the attention he wants. But it's not an issue of God's insecurity. It's an issue of God's supremacy. It is the economics of glory. When man's glory is raised against God's, the bottom line of the riches of God's glory reveals the utter bankruptcy of man's. These texts are warnings given to kings and nations who can't do the math of the universe and have miscalculated their significance and power to the intentional neglect of ascribing to God his immeasurable value. They rejoice in the work of their hands, the brilliance of their plans, and the displays of their power, intentionally oblivious and indifferent to the surpassing greatness, brilliance, and power of God.

Imagine attending the 2014 New Year's fireworks show in Dubai, which, at a cost of nearly six million dollars, was the largest the world has ever seen. As you gaze into the sky in amazement, feeling the rumblings in your chest from the explosions, some kid yanks on your pant leg and tries to sell you a ticket for a viewing of the Roman candle he is about to set off. He's cute, but he's confused and has missed the point. His Roman candle is laughable and will barely be visible in the glow of six million dollars' worth of fireworks. This is what God is getting at and what the prophet Isaiah is helping us see. We are the glory hogs with our little Roman candles; God's just a realist.

In John 12, just before John indicts the religious leaders for their glory hunger, he makes a staggering statement about Jesus:

> Though he had done so many signs before them, they still did not believe in him, so that the word spoken by the prophet Isaiah might be fulfilled: "Lord, who has believed what he heard from us, and to whom has the arm of the Lord been revealed?" Therefore they could not believe. For again Isaiah said, "He has blinded their eyes and hardened their heart, lest they see with their eyes, and understand with their heart, and turn, and I would heal them." Isaiah said these things because he saw his glory and spoke of him. (John 12:37–41)

The unrivaled glory that Isaiah saw and rejoiced in was none other than the glory of Jesus. John, in this passage, identifies Jesus with Yahweh of the Old Testament. Jesus is the eternal one, God the Son, one with the Father, possessing equal glory and power. In the prologue to John's Gospel, he tells us that God the Son, the Word, "became flesh and dwelt among us, and we have seen his glory, glory as of the only Son from the Father, full of grace and truth" (1:14). Jesus brought glory into focus, and it was stunning; a glory full of grace and faithfulness. That is the kind of glory we want exalted in the end and the kind that will be exalted in the end. When the Scriptures speak of the Lord alone being exalted in that day, it speaks of none other than Jesus Christ. The ancient hymn of Philippians 2 identifies Jesus as God incarnate, the humble servant, crucified, risen, and exalted by the Father and given the highest name:

> Have this mind among yourselves, which is yours in Christ Jesus, who, though he was in the form of God, did not count equality with God a thing to be grasped, but emptied himself, by taking the form of a servant, being born in the likeness of men. And being found in human form, he humbled himself by becoming obedient to the point of death, even death on a cross. Therefore God has highly exalted him and bestowed on him the name that is above every name, so that at the name of Jesus every knee should bow, in heaven and on earth and under the earth, and every tongue confess that Jesus Christ is Lord, to the glory of God the Father. (Phil. 2:5–11)

Jesus possesses a name that is higher than any other, and the world is destined to acknowledge it. That truth is the ultimate end of every single person. When the smoke clears and the dust settles, only one person in the cosmos is left standing; everyone else is kneeling. Some will kneel to their eternal joy, and some will kneel to their eternal sorrow, but all will kneel. On that day, the lofty pride of men will be brought low.

Listen to how the apostle Paul describes the risen and exalted Christ:

> He is the image of the invisible God, the firstborn of all creation. For by him all things were created, in heaven and on earth, visible and invisible, whether thrones or dominions or

rulers or authorities—all things were created through him and for him. And he is before all things, and in him all things hold together. And he is the head of the body, the church. He is the beginning, the firstborn from the dead, that in everything he might be preeminent. (Col. 1:15–18)

The historical Jesus of the small village of Nazareth is the creator of all things, seen and unseen. And he holds all things together, and all things are destined to honor him. Every created thing exists to make much of him. He is the eternal one, incarnate, crucified, risen, exalted, reigning, and returning so that in *everything* he might be preeminent. We don't use that word, *preeminent*, much today, but it means to possess first place in all things at all times. It means to have a superior status in every domain. Jesus is the preeminent one. He is the only one with that on his resume.

In 1966 John Lennon commented to the American press that the Beatles were more popular than Jesus. He may have been right. There is a difference between being preeminent and being popular. There are people in the world who do not know about Jesus, but they recognize the names and pictures of NBA stars. There are many who do not know the story of Jesus, but they know the song lyrics of musical artists. Many people surpass Jesus in popularity.

For Christmas one year, my wife and I took our teenage daughter to see one of her favorite artists in concert. The arena was packed, mainly with middle-school girls. When the star of the show made her grand entrance, the crowd erupted. After the first song, she stood center stage to the sound of deafening shouts. As she turned her gaze to one side of the arena, the applause and cheers of those sitting in that particular section exploded. Then she turned her gaze to the other side, and the crowd screamed at even higher decibels. This went on for about two minutes. I was stunned at the immensity of her popularity, and I nearly lost my voice.

The preeminence of Jesus is an unseen reality but will one day become visible. The center stage of the cosmos belongs to Jesus, and one day he will take it in a visible, undeniable, irreversible way to the joyful shouts of angels and nations and the unending wail of all who have refused him.

My family has a little chalkboard that hangs up on one of our walls. Written on that board is one of our family mantras that we seek to embody in our attitudes and actions. The chalkboard reads, "Jesus is King, not I." My temptation, and yours too, I might add, is to deny that reality and live with myself enthroned in my heart. The great temptation of the glory-hungry masses is to think and act as if our show is the most pressing reality of life. We buy into the lie that if we can have center stage and bask in the approval of fans and admirers, then we will be truly happy. But the truth is, your happiness depends upon your conforming to reality. If you are to be happy, you must write, "Jesus is King, not I," over your life—not in chalk but in stone. David Naugle is helpful at this point:

> Those who have studied the history of the idea of happiness in a Western context have observed how it migrated from its original home in religion and philosophy to the political sphere and, most recently, into the domain of individual experience. Classically, among the great western philosophers and theologians, happiness denoted the state of the genuine fulfillment of human nature that resulted from being properly related as a person to the truth of reality. Educating the soul to conform it to reality, rather than conforming reality to the dictates of the individual soul, was the secret to the happy life. But those days of defining happiness and the good life, and what it means to be truly human, are long gone.[26]

The unwavering focus on self as an attempt to secure happiness is futile, because it is not properly related to reality. In Jesus's most famous sermon, he said that the happy ones are the poor in spirit, those who have seen the world for what it is and removed themselves from the center of it. The happy ones are the humble ones who have renounced self-focus, self-promotion, and self-reliance. They have surrendered to the reality of every knee bowing and every tongue confessing the uncontested, unrivaled, unmatched glory of the Lord Jesus. This is how the universe works. It is an unchanging, irrevocable reality.

It's imperative that we contemplate this truth; otherwise we run the risk of exhausting ourselves, building up what one day will be torn down. Think about it in business terms. Would you invest your life savings in a company you knew would go bankrupt in just a short time? Would you invest all your money in renovating an apartment for which you only had a one-year lease? To invest fully in what is transient is the ultimate bad investment. To exalt ourselves is to run against the grain of the universe, and it is the surest way to sabotage our life and joy.

It might be that self-glory seeking is not the sustained posture of your heart or the trajectory of your life but that there are consistent patterns and traces of it. Personally, on a big-picture level, I know and delight in the preeminence of Jesus and have yielded my life to that reality. But on a granular level, I still find myself competing with Jesus for glory. I do things Jesus desires with motivations Jesus despises. His words about the scribes disturb me:

> Beware of the scribes, who like to walk around in long robes, and love greetings in the marketplaces and the best seats in the synagogues and the places of honor at feasts. (Luke 20:46)

The scribes were glory hungry. They engaged in religious work but wanted to be honored, esteemed, recognized, and noticed. They were motivated by the glory that came from the crowds. Their ministries were their stages, and they loved the applause of the crowds. I can relate to that. I want to speak truth, but I want to be quoted for the profound way I say it. I want to preach faithfully, but I also want to be invited and downloaded as a gifted preacher. I want to see the church I serve grow, but I want to be showcased for that growth. I compete with Jesus for glory.

In the middle of 2013, I was facing the decision of whether to leave my ministry in New York City. During that time a friend and counselor said to me, "JR, there are sinful reasons to leave New York, but there are also some sinful reasons to stay." I felt that God had made clear to me that my time there was done, and I was to submit to him concerning what he had next for me, my family, and our church. Yet as I reflected on my friend's statement, it dawned on me how much of my decision was clouded by my glory hunger. I was in arguably the most important city in North America, maybe the world, pastoring a thriving and growing church we had planted eight years prior. Planting that church had become my badge of honor. My identity and sense of importance were wrapped up in it. I too much enjoyed being recognized, esteemed, and applauded for our "bold move" to the city. I enjoyed the powerful context full of important people who shape the culture and determine the future of vocational domains. If I left New York, I feared I would be merely normal, average, ordinary—and forgotten. I was in bondage to my glory, and I was in competition with Jesus for his glory.

Graciously and gradually God set me free from that bondage and brought me to repentance and allowed me to divorce my identity from my ministry and zip code. He took me back to the gospel of Jesus, where I find my identity as the beloved of God. He overwhelmed all my fears of being forgotten by convincing me that it's much better to have my name graven on Jesus's hands than up in lights. And he took me back to the glory of Jesus, moving me backstage where I can see a little more clearly his brilliance and preeminence. Now I sit here writing a book on glory hunger in a small, borrowed, upstairs office of a tire shop and lube center in a small East Texas town. And as I prepare for what God has next for me, I can say that the gospel and glory of Jesus have freed me from the need for it to be awesome, visible, or noteworthy. I feel that I'm going with the grain of the universe. And there is joy in that.

The battle is not over for me. It is not over for any of us. Whether we are kings like the ones Isaiah confronted or workers for minimum wage, we will wrestle with glory hunger that competes with God for praise. So, practically, what can we do to maintain a posture and trajectory consistent with the grain of the universe?

Listen to What the Cross Says about You

The vantage point of the cross of Jesus will always give us the best perspective about ourselves. Paul, whose accomplishments are rivaled only by Jesus himself, would boast in nothing but the cross (Gal. 6:14). It defined his life. To him, nothing spoke louder over his life than the cross. When we listen to it, it humbles us. John Stott writes:

> Every time we look at the cross Christ seems to say to us, "I am here because of you. It is your sin I am bearing, your curse I am suffering, your debt I am paying, your death I am dying." Nothing in history or in the universe cuts us down to size like the cross. All of us have inflated views of ourselves, especially in self-righteousness, until we have visited a place called Calvary. It is there, at the foot of the cross, that we shrink to our true size.[27]

The cross forces self-awareness upon us. It speaks the worst things that could ever be said about us. If pride is rising up in me over my accomplishments, strengths, or reputation, the cross says, "You are weak, powerless, foolish, selfish, lustful, lying, God belittling, and neighbor neglecting, and even your best acts are tainted with wrong motives and are filthy rags before God." The cross deflates us and serves as a clarifying lens that allows us to see our true condition. When we are tempted to boast in ourselves, the cross tells us that we are not awesome.

Yet the cross also tells us that despite how not awesome we are, God loves us and wants us. The cross will plunge us to the depths of humility, causing us to put our hand over our mouths and silence our praise of self, and it will lift us to the heights, causing us to open our mouths in praise to God for his grace. The cross strips us of glory and at the same time bestows a more glorious glory upon us. When you are tempted to think highly of yourself, remind yourself why Jesus had to die. Let the cross measure you, not your accomplishments, or your failures for that matter.

Remember from Where Your Blessings Come

When God rescued Israel from Egypt and was on the brink of bringing them into the Promised Land, he warned them of the effect that his blessings could have upon them. He was going to richly provide for them, blessing them with food, houses, herds, flocks, silver, gold, and everything they would need to flourish. He warned them that in that place of prosperity, they would run the risk of forgetting the God who had brought them there. The danger was that their hearts would be lifted up in pride, and they would credit themselves for all their wealth, possessions, and success. So God commanded them:

> Beware lest you say in your heart, "My power and the might of my hand have gotten me this wealth." You shall remember the LORD your God, for it is he who gives you power to get wealth, that he may confirm his covenant that he swore to your fathers, as it is this day. And if you forget the LORD your God and go

after other gods and serve them and worship them, I solemnly warn you today that you shall surely perish. (Deut. 8:17–19)

The most common way we compete with God for glory is by thinking that somehow we are ultimately responsible for the success and any measure of prosperity we might have. To be clear, God affirms excellence. The proverbs tell us that if we are skilled in our work, we won't stand before obscure people but before kings (Prov. 22:29). We should seek to honor God with diligence and excellence. But when we credit our intelligence, our strength, our tenacity, or our talents for the good things we enjoy or the success we experience, we have become glory robbers, and God will humble us. We fight our glory hunger by remembering who butters our bread and who gave us the bread in the first place. This is what God wanted to teach the arrogant king of Assyria:

> When the Lord has finished all his work on Mount Zion and on Jerusalem, he will punish the speech of the arrogant heart of the king of Assyria and the boastful look in his eyes. For he says:
>
> By the strength of my hand I have done it,
>> and by my wisdom, for I have understanding;
> I remove the boundaries of peoples,
>> and plunder their treasures;
>> like a bull I bring down those who sit on thrones.
> My hand has found like a nest
>> the wealth of the peoples;
> and as one gathers eggs that have been forsaken,
>> so I have gathered all the earth;
> and there was none that moved a wing
>> or opened the mouth or chirped. (Isa. 10:12–14)

The king of Assyria revealed his arrogant heart in taking credit for the expanse of his rule. He was impressed with his wisdom and understanding and with the strength of his hands. The king was failing to acknowledge what the Scriptures are replete with, namely, that God rules the affairs of the world, and kings and kingdoms are instruments in his hands to accomplish his purpose for his glory:

> Shall the axe boast over him who hews with it,
>   or the saw magnify itself against him who wields it?
> As if a rod should wield him who lifts it,
>   or as if a staff should lift him who is not wood!
> Therefore the Lord GOD of hosts
>   will send wasting sickness among his stout warriors,
> and under his glory a burning will be kindled,
>   like the burning of fire. (Isa. 10:15–16)

We are mere instruments in the Lord's hands. When we praise ourselves, we are like the axe who thinks that by its power the tree fell. He wields us for his purposes, and it is foolish to boast over him or magnify ourselves against him by taking credit for what he is doing through us. We can acknowledge that we are privileged to be the Lord's instruments and that we are thrilled to be found faithful in the endeavors he chooses to accomplish through us, but to try to pick the pocket of God in an attempt to steal his glory will end poorly. There is no such thing as a self-made man.

Paul, who unquestionably had a tremendous ministry and a large area of influence, understood this. He refused to take credit for the Lord's work through him. He could honestly say that he worked harder than anyone else in the ministry but that it was the grace of God, not his strength or talent, that brought about the results. Whatever he was, he was that because of the grace of God at work within him (1 Cor. 15:10).

In the book of Acts, we get a case study of one who sought to exalt himself above Jesus. King Herod Agrippa I violently opposed the church. As Acts 12 opens, King Herod has beheaded the apostle James, imprisoned Peter, and laid violent hands on other Christians. However, by the end of Acts 12 Peter is free, the gospel is multiplying, and God has struck Herod dead, not for stealing James's life but for something that God deemed even worse—attempting to steal his glory:

> On an appointed day Herod put on his royal robes, took his seat upon the throne, and delivered an oration to them. And the people were shouting, "The voice of a god, and not of a man!" Immediately an angel of the Lord struck him down, because he did not give God the glory, and he was eaten by worms and breathed his last. (Acts 12:21–23)

Could Herod Agrippa's biography have ended any worse? He was a glory hog and gorged himself to death. Two chapters later, we get a picture of two people so smitten with the glory of God that competing with him for praise was unthinkable. Paul and Barnabas entered Lystra and begin to preach the gospel. Upon encountering a crippled man, they healed him. It was such a powerful moment that the people of Lystra began to shout, "The gods have come down to us in the likeness of men!" (14:11). What a compliment to the glory hungry! Not so for Paul and Barnabas. When they heard that the people were calling them gods and wanting to sacrifice animals to them, they tore their garments and rushed out into the crowd yelling,

> Men, why are you doing these things? We also are men, of like nature with you, and we bring you good news, that you should turn from these vain things to a living God, who made the heaven and the earth and the sea and all that is in them. (v. 15)

Who are we that we should receive praise? We are created; God is the creator. We are always the recipients; he is always the giver. We must fight to remember that every blessing, every strength, every joy, every victory, and all of our wealth, wisdom, and worth is from him. He is the fountain of all goodness. This means that we must cultivate the habit of giving praise to him for every good thing, big and small. When gratitude is the knee-jerk reaction to the graces God bestows on us, we cease competing with God for glory. Entitlement says, "I deserved it." Pride says, "I did it." Gratitude says, "I received it."

We must also cultivate the art of deflecting praise that comes from others, learning to receive encouragement without our hearts hoarding the credit. I'm not suggesting that every time someone compliments us for an achievement, we make them uncomfortable with our, "Oh, it wasn't me; it was God. All praise and glory go to him." Actually, if it were all God, it would have turned out a lot better than what you did. God accomplished something, and you played a part. As a pastor, when someone compliments me on a sermon, I have learned to say, "Thank you so much for that encouragement. I'm glad the Lord could use the sermon in your life." I had a part to play in God's work in their life, but it was God's work. I know that I may plant or water, but God is the one who gives growth and makes my efforts fruitful, and ultimately only he deserves the praise (1 Cor. 3:6–7). We can receive compliments without giving into self-congratulatory ways. It always amuses me when people on Twitter re-tweet compliments posted about them by others. Such "look at me" self-promotional ways run contrary to a heart that has learned to ask, "Who am I, Lord?" In short, we have to learn to rend our hearts like Paul tore his clothes when we are faced with the risk of robbing God.

Practice the Discipline of Obscurity

Obscurity is a dreaded word but a helpful discipline for Jesus's people who want to battle their glory hunger. Jesus addressed this in the Sermon on the Mount, where he warned his followers about "practicing your righteousness before other people in order to be seen by them" (Matt. 6:1). There is nothing wrong with being seen doing the things that God commands and encourages. Jesus told his listeners earlier in the sermon that if they live as he calls them to live, people will see it and glorify God for it (Matt. 5:16). However, Jesus knows that our glory hunger can turn us into religious performers. Jesus tells us that if we do things primarily to be seen by people, that is the reward we get. Not only is God grieved by it, but we lose, forfeiting a reward greater than the approving glances of people.

The way Jesus encourages us to battle our glory hunger is to retreat into the obscure place and practice our righteousness in invisible ways. Pray in the closet. Give without announcing it. Fast without making it obvious to others that you are fasting. Engage in acts of covert service or generosity in ways that no one sees or hears about, especially from you. In today's social media–crazed world, this must be intentional. We can declare war against ourselves in our glory war against God by embracing intentional obscurity and secrecy.

Don't tweet about your devotional time. Don't tweet a prayer request for someone with whom you just shared the gospel, when you know you want admiration as much as you want the sinner's conversion. Pastors and ministry leaders, don't post your ministry successes or how many people attended your church or event, when you know deep down that you want to be envied for it. Many need to fast from social media altogether.

Spiritual directors often encourage people to embrace the discipline of silence for the sake of self-examination. Silence can reveal to us how we often use our words for reputation building and reputation management. Silence helps us renounce that tendency and can be a means of grace that the Holy Spirit uses to free us from our addiction to self. It might be that social-media silence is more revealing. Many of us would benefit from taking an extended break from it. You might discover how natural your impulse is to talk about yourself and to check if anyone "likes" or retweets what you have said.

Embrace obscurity by doing your best to raise and praise other people. It is natural to have a zero-sum-game mentality when it comes to glory. And these zero-sum-game mind-sets can be brutal. How many times have you seen others throw a team member under the bus to avoid looking bad or to make themselves look good in hope of promotion? When we buy into that mind-set, we work to take as much credit as we can. To subvert this credit-mongering glory hunger, we need to raise and praise other people. Look for ways to spread out the credit. Look for ways to give other people the opportunity to succeed. If you are a team leader, share decision making, praising others when they make good decisions and sharing the responsibility when they don't. If you are a pastor, share your pulpit and publicly praise staff and volunteers for their contributions that make the church function and thrive.

Conclusion

The happiest people are those who are most free from personal glory hunger and refuse to compete with God for glory. They see themselves from the vantage point of the cross and possess an accurate self-awareness of their weakness and depravity. They are content with the unearned love shown to them there. They are running with the grain of the universe, keeping in step with ultimate reality. They acknowledge that all they have comes from God. They gladly confess it is by his power and grace that any good comes to them or is displayed through them. This takes on a horizontal dimension in their lives as well. They proactively look for ways to see others honored for the way God is at work in their lives. They delight to see God using other people to accomplish his purposes. They are not threatened by the success of others but are able to attribute it to God and submit to his wisdom in it. And when they feel their glory hunger rising up and gnawing at them, they embrace obscurity, claiming it as a friend in their battle against the formidable foe of pride.

7

Losing Glory
to Gain It

My family loves to take long road trips. Every trek is a bonding experience—at least that is what I keep telling myself. I don't remember much about long road trips I took as a kid other than, as the baby of the family, I was usually in the backseat, in the middle, with my feet uncomfortably positioned between the sides of the humpback floorboard. However, I do recall from one road trip my first exposure to our nation's blue laws. It was a Sunday afternoon, and my mom pulled over to buy a paring knife to peel and slice some fruit we had brought along for snacks. I distinctly remember my mom coming back to the car empty-handed, the sales clerk refusing to sell her the knife because it was a Sunday and the state's blue laws would not allow it.

Originally, blue laws forced the closure of stores on Sundays. The laws were motivated not by a concern for workers' need for rest but in honor of the Christian Sabbath. Blue laws were intended to enforce the observance of Sunday as a day of worship and rest. In 1854 the state of New Jersey enacted these blue laws. One writer quotes an 1879 article from the *New York Times* and describes the restrictions:

> The Sunday laws of New-Jersey provide that no traveling, worldly employment or business, ordinary or servile work on

lawn or water, (works of charity or necessity alone excepted) shall be done or performed on the Christian Sabbath. It is also provided that no goods or chattels shall be exposed for sale or vended, as meat, fruit, fish, herbs, milk or vegetables; nor shall anyone travel on that day, except when going to or from church, or going for a physician, surgeon, or mid-wife, or in the service of the United States mail carriage.[28]

In 1885 the Supreme Court upheld these laws not to promote religion but to prevent unnecessary physical labor. In the early twentieth century certain exemptions were allowed, and the blue laws were increasingly relaxed. However, many states still exercise the laws, not permitting the sale of alcohol, vehicles, or other goods on a Sunday. In fact, New Jersey's Bergen County still restricts Sunday shopping. In the aftermath of Hurricane Sandy, New Jersey Governor Chris Christie suspended the blue laws, instigating quite a legal battle.

If you consider the existence of blue laws, it's clear that Christianity has held a place of privilege in the West, particularly in America. In previous decades, Christian beliefs strongly shaped the majority mind-set, and Christian ethics served as the benchmark for societal morality. One cause of the church's privileged position was the conversion of Emperor Constantine.

The genuineness of Constantine's conversion is obviously doubted; nonetheless, his conversion set in motion the emergence of a Western world that favored the Christian church and gave it a privileged place in society. A worldview known as "Christendom," or "Constantinianism," was born, and with it the world began to shift. The Christian story became widely known, and the Christian Scriptures became authoritative. Structures, systems, and laws were put in place that favored the church and its appointed leaders.

The church emerged as the dominant controlling power and

cultural influencer in the Middle Ages. Church leaders (who were sometimes corrupt) held places of prominence, wealth, and dominance in society, and this focus on glory and privilege removed the radical nature of following Jesus. Wanting power and position contradicted the theology of the cross, and the radical nature of discipleship was lost. The line that separated true followers of Jesus from merely professing adherents meeting cultural expectations became very blurred. Baptism was more of a cultural expectation than a visible identification with a suffering Messiah to whom one pledged dying loyalty and love.

That social construct lasted for millennia. Yet decades ago it all began to change. Stanley Hauerwas and William Willimon, in their book *Resident Aliens*, recall how in 1963, in defiance of their state's blue laws, the Fox Theater in Greenville, South Carolina, opened on Sunday. Before then, the church had been the only show in town on Sundays.

> In taking a child to Sunday school, parents affirmed everything that was good, wholesome, reasonable and American. Church, home and the state formed a national consortium that worked together to instill "Christian values."[29]

Referring to the night the Fox Theater opened, Hauerwas and Willimon called it a "watershed in the history of Christendom":

> On that night Greenville, SC—that last pocket of resistance to secularity in the Western world—served notice that it would no longer be a prop for the church. There would be no more free passes for the church, no more free rides. The Fox Theater went head to head with the church over who would provide the worldview for the young. That night in 1963, the Fox Theater won the opening skirmish. . . . We in no way mean to imply that, before 1963, things were better for believers. Our point

is that, before the Fox Theater opened on Sunday, Christians could deceive themselves into thinking that we were in charge, that we had made a difference, that we had created a Christian culture.[30]

In the world of Christendom, the church held a voice in the mores and values and life practices of the culture. Not so anymore. We no longer live in Christendom; we live in a post-Constantinian, post-Christian culture. In most places in our country, prayer has been removed from schools, the Ten Commandments are no longer displayed in public venues, and nativity scenes are casualties in the "war on Christmas." Increasingly, Christians are finding themselves less at home in the culture. As the West, in particular, becomes increasingly secular, Christians are finding themselves on the "wrong side" of some of the issues that matter most to the culture. In fact, the more Christians hold to a biblical vision of human life and nature, human sexuality, and the uniqueness and exclusivity of Jesus, we will be branded as the morally reprehensible who stand in the way of social progress.

We have seen over the last several years an outrage from the culture toward Christians over our biblical convictions. At President Obama's 2012 inauguration, a prominent pastor was invited to give the invocation but was cut from the program after a small but vocal organization demanded his removal. They discovered a sermon he had preached nearly two decades before in which he categorized homosexuality as a sin and a violation of God's intention for human sexuality. The outrage over his statements led to his dismissal. At the inauguration, not one evangelical Christian was on the program.

Christians today face the real prospect of the diminishing of religious freedom. As public policies are put in place, Christians who own businesses are fighting and filing lawsuits, seeking to operate according to personal consciences held captive by the Scriptures.

We live in a culture that requires the unconditional affirmation of individual moral choices and threatens legal action against anyone who will not acquiesce.

This atmosphere is only going to grow increasingly more hostile. Christians need to fight to preserve and protect the religious freedoms of all people, but we need not fight to bring back Christendom or to gain a place of privilege. We don't need to long for the "good ole days," because in many ways those days were not good. They were a smokescreen for the real status of nominal Christians. The current cultural context actually provides us a tremendous opportunity to reveal authentic disciples and to recapture the original flavor of discipleship.

The Bible has a lot to say about being disciples of Jesus in a context like this. In particular, the apostle Peter's first letter carries significant relevance. It was written to a group of Christians scattered throughout what is now Turkey. They lived in what we would call a "pre-Christian" era. It was a time marked by pluralism and emperor worship and hostility toward Christianity. The church of Jesus did not have a privileged place in society. They were marginalized, looked upon with suspicion, and persecuted. As we read Peter's first letter, we see that the church was spoken against and its adherents slandered as evildoers (2:12; 3:18). They faced threats of physical suffering (4:1); they were maligned (4:4), insulted (4:14), and treated unjustly (2:19).

In that cultural context, your baptism meant something, not just theologically but also sociologically. Following Jesus meant a loss of social standing and cultural currency. If you were going to step out and declare your faith in Jesus, you ran the risk of ridicule, suffering, marginalization, and loss—all the things a glory-hungry culture flinches at. These are not the perks that provide incentive to those who are ambitious for approval. Yet these first-century Christians enthusiastically embraced Jesus and the social ramifications that came along with belonging to him. Many people in our culture would rather die before losing face or experiencing the social ostracism that followers of Jesus in a pre-Christian era encountered. As Peter wrote his letter, he did not encourage the church to fight for the social center or seek to gain a place of privilege but to embrace their identity as exiles:

> Peter, an apostle of Jesus Christ, To those who are elect *exiles* of the Dispersion in Pontus, Galatia, Cappadocia, Asia, and Bithynia. (1 Pet. 1:1)

Peter called those believers exiles and sojourners in this world (1 Pet. 1:1; 2:11). They were citizens of the kingdom of God and no longer in sync with the world. As followers of Jesus, we can expect a disconnect and an unsettledness. We should not quite be at home here. We are resident aliens, living in this world but with another world burning in our hearts.

Peter's reference to "exiles of the Dispersion" was a technical term used to describe Jews living outside of Palestine. By the first century there were Jews living all over the Roman world, and diaspora communities had formed in major cities. Those communities maintained their Jewish identity. They established synagogues, celebrated the feasts, observed Sabbath, studied and obeyed the Torah, sent a temple tax back to Jerusalem, and even invited Gentiles into their community to become worshipers of God. While away from Jerusalem and the temple, they lived with the temple in their hearts and sought to remain faithful to their identity as worshipers of God, even while on foreign soil among a culture that worshiped idols and emperors. They wanted to be faithful to God in the midst of a culture that embraced ways of living that were radically deviant from what God had revealed to be his will for his people.

Peter did not use the word *diaspora* in a literal sense. He was writing his letter to Gentiles. Rather, he used the word to speak of his Christian readers (which includes us) and to say, "You are a community of God's people living on foreign soil whose vision of reality, and whose values, passions, purposes, and life patterns differ radically from the host culture. You are a peculiar people, different, odd, not at home here. You are the faithful worshipers of God in a land that does not know God. So even as you seek to introduce others to your God, prepare to experience the awkwardness of living out of step with the culture. Prepare for rejection, loss, ridicule, suffering, and marginalization. Prepare to lose the glory and esteem that come from men. If you follow Jesus, and if you give yourself to his mission, you are going to have to take it on the social chin."

As we see Peter pastor those first-century Christians, his letter is valuable to those of us who wrestle with glory hunger and crave people's approval. We face the temptation to turn down the volume on our faith. A post-Christian mind-set has relegated faith to the private life of values and ideas and sought to remove it from the public realm of facts. We are tempted to cower before this mind-set and privatize our faith. In a world that laughs at the church's convictions and values, it becomes socially safer to hide in the shadows and distance ourselves from the church. We face the constant pressure to compromise convictions in order to stay in the good graces of friends and strangers who reject our faith and our understanding of reality. We don't want to be excluded or rejected; it hurts. It is normal to avoid pain, so we lean toward guarding ourselves against criticism. If we speak our convictions regarding areas that are culturally off-limits, we face being denounced as unloving, bigoted, narrow-minded, or judgmental. We find ourselves in a situation similar to that of the men in John 12:42–43 who would not confess Jesus for fear of social consequences. There are people who once walked with Jesus who today no longer openly confess him because the glory that comes from people means too much to them. It cannot be risked.

To encourage bold and unabashed faithfulness to Jesus in the face of loss, Peter first reminds his original audience (and us, his modern readers) of how God feels about them, how he feels about Jesus, and what he promises in the end to the faithful:

> Peter, an apostle of Jesus Christ, To those who are elect exiles of the Dispersion in Pontus, Galatia, Cappadocia, Asia, and Bithynia, according to the foreknowledge of God the Father, in the sanctification of the Spirit, for obedience to Jesus Christ and for sprinkling with his blood: May grace and peace be multiplied to you. (1 Pet. 1:1–2)

They are the elect of God, chosen by God, called out by God. Don't miss the big idea here because you want to swim in its intricate theological complications. God is always the pursuer. God comes after us with mercy and grace. He always initiates; we don't. If you are a Christian, being called "elect" means that you are a Christian because it was God's design all along to call you and personally draw you to Christ and make you his son or daughter. And the Scriptures tell us that he chose you to be his before you could do anything that would make you marketable or desirable:

> Blessed be the God and Father of our Lord Jesus Christ, who has blessed us in Christ with every spiritual blessing in the heavenly places, even as he chose us in him before the foundation of the world, that we should be holy and blameless before him. In love he predestined us for adoption as sons through Jesus Christ, according to the purpose of his will, to the praise of his glorious grace, with which he has blessed us in the Beloved. (Eph. 1:3–6)

He chose you out of sheer love, before the world even began, according to the purpose of his will and for the praise and magnification of his glorious grace. In salvation, we don't initiate, create, or contribute—it is all God from beginning to end. We don't convince God to take us; he convinces us to come to him. We don't desire him and then melt his resistance to us; he desires us and melts our resistance to him. We don't overcome his unwillingness; he overcomes ours.

If you believe in Jesus today, it is because God determined to bring you to himself and to give himself fully to you. Left to ourselves we would never give ourselves completely to him. It is his doing that we know him (1 Cor. 1:30; Gal. 4:9). This means that you did not keep God at bay and then at some point inform him that he could come into your life. Rather, he laid hold of you when he wanted and brought you into his life. Peter teaches us that the entire community of the Trinity—Father, Son, and Holy Spirit—is intimately involved in bringing about this great work of saving you and making you part of the divine family.

Our election is according to the foreknowledge of God the Father. This means more than that the Father had previous knowledge that you would trust in Jesus. In the Scripture, "foreknowledge" refers to God's settled plan to set his love upon individuals and bring them into relationship with himself. It is the Father saying, "I choose to love you with a saving love. I am determined at great cost to myself to deal with every obstacle standing in the way of our relationship, and I have determined to win your heart with that saving love and be a Father to you." The Father architects salvation.

The Son shed his blood for our salvation. The Father sent his eternal Son from his side to take on full humanity to die for the sins of those the Father determined to save. He shed his blood to provide forgiveness of sins and remove the insurmountable obstacle standing between the Father and us. The Son accomplished salvation.

The Spirit sanctifies us. He sets us apart to belong to Jesus. He opens our eyes to who Jesus is and works faith in our hearts so that we come to Jesus for life. The Holy Spirit introduces us to Jesus, the Son, and intimately connects us to him by faith so that all the benefits of the Son's life, death, and resurrection become ours. So the Spirit applies salvation.

The entirety of the divine community has mobilized to bring about your salvation and eternal joy. We have to hear this as the first-century church in a pre-Christian culture heard it, a church that was suffering, facing conflict, and living in an environment that was hostile to their faith. They were despised by the world, but they were deeply loved and chosen by the Father. They were marginal in society, but they were in the center of God's saving purposes. They were discarded by the world as worthless, but they were purchased by the precious blood of God's Son, a currency far more valuable than gold or silver (1 Pet. 1:18–19).

Like them, we have been on God's heart from eternity and still are. He loves us, prizes us, and has gone to great lengths to secure us for himself. He is deeply invested in us, has not forgotten us, and will not forsake us. He is a trustworthy God, who loves us with a steadfast love. Our life is in his hands, and, ultimately, whatever challenges we face, God will work them all out for our joy in the end. The Godhead, the divine community, from all eternity has determined to have us and to do good to us forever.

So no matter how this world feels about you, rest in how God feels about you. No matter what this world says about you, listen to what God says about you. You are his people, objects of his love and mercy, valued and precious to him (1 Pet. 2:9–10). Make the opinion of the one who matters most, matter most to you. When you are content in his acceptance, you can face any rejection. No matter what this world threatens against you, rest in what God has promised to you.

Second, Peter reminds them about the glory of Jesus and how the Father feels about him:

> As you come to him, a living stone rejected by men but in the sight of God chosen and precious, you yourselves like living stones are being built up as a spiritual house, to be a holy priesthood, to offer spiritual sacrifices acceptable to God through Jesus Christ. For it stands in Scripture: "Behold, I am laying in Zion a stone, a cornerstone chosen and precious, and whoever believes in him will not be put to shame." (1 Pet. 2:4–6)

Jesus was rejected by men. He was betrayed by one of his followers, denied by another, falsely condemned by a mockery of a court, abandoned by friends, beaten by cruel people who did not fear God, and humiliatingly crucified like a common criminal. That is how the world felt about Jesus. It is still how the world feels about Jesus. But to God, Jesus is choice and precious. The Father esteems Jesus.

When Peter calls Jesus "a living stone," he is speaking of his resurrection. Jesus's trial and crucifixion were humanity's verdict on Jesus. The resurrection was God's vindication of Jesus. Through his life, death, and resurrection God made him both Savior and Lord, exalted him to the highest place, and gave him all rule and dominion. Humanity cast him away as an insignificant pebble, but God exalted him as the cornerstone. Peter uses an image of the stone in a building that is laid first and by which all other stones are oriented. In other words, Jesus is the most important figure of human history, the centerpiece of God's plan for this world. Rejected by men but chosen and precious to God; humiliated by men but honored by God. In the end, the only honor that will be handed out is to Jesus and to those who have sided with God in his estimation of Jesus.

We can expect the same treatment from the world that those in Peter's day experienced. Jesus taught us that our identification with him will mean being hated by the world. If the world persecuted Jesus, we can be certain that it will persecute us, his followers. The servants aren't above their master. In parts of the world this means imprisonment and even death. According to the Pew Research Center, in 2012 social hostility, violence, and discrimination increased in nearly every region of the world, with the exception of the Americas.[31] Currently, in the United States we do not face imprisonment or death for our faith, but Jesus's words regarding the cost of identifying with him still ring true. Holding to Jesus and biblical convictions can cost you a job promotion, an election, or a lawsuit. Confronting radical individualism and advocating God's vision in the most intimate matters of human life can often get you demonized and vilified as a hateful bigot. Some Christians invite these labels with behavior that is less than winsome and wise, but many believers with a humble and compassionate posture are met with hostility when verbalizing their convictions. We should not be shocked by this or pout about it. Jesus did not pull a bait-and-switch on us; he was clear about this from the start.

When our glory hunger tempts us to privatize our faith in order to preserve our honor before people, we have lost sight of the worth and preeminence of Jesus and have valued our reputation above his. Our failure to unashamedly align with Jesus on the most sensitive matters of our day through fear of losing face betrays a gross underestimate of the worth of Jesus. When we avoid taking Jesus-honoring postures on lightning-rod issues so as to manage our public relations, we have overvalued our relationship with the public and undervalued our relationship with Jesus. We have lost sight of how precious Jesus is to the Father and of the honor God has bestowed upon him. But we have also lost sight of the honor God promises to those who share his estimation of Jesus in consequential ways.

Third, Peter wants to point his readers' gaze forward to the hope of the glory that is to be revealed to them:

> Blessed be the God and Father of our Lord Jesus Christ! According to his great mercy, he has caused us to be born again to a living hope through the resurrection of Jesus Christ from the dead, to an inheritance that is imperishable, undefiled, and unfading, kept in heaven for you, who by God's power are being guarded through faith for a salvation ready to be revealed in the last time. In this you rejoice, though now for a little while, if necessary, you have been grieved by various trials, so that the tested genuineness of your faith—more precious than gold that perishes though it is tested by fire—may be found to result in praise and glory and honor at the revelation of Jesus Christ. Though you have not seen him, you love him. Though you do not now see him, you believe in him and rejoice with joy that is inexpressible and filled with glory, obtaining the outcome of your faith, the salvation of your souls. (1 Pet. 1:3–9)

Not all glory hunger is bad. Living for transient, fading glory that comes from people is futile bondage. But God motivates us with a glory that is eternal, lasting, and infinitely more satisfying than the dim, imitation glory that comes from men.

Peter describes this future hope as "an inheritance," language borrowed from the Old Testament promises to God's people that spoke of a promised land of prosperity and peace and rest from all their enemies. The Promised Land was a living illustration of the final salvation that God has planned for his people in the new heavens and the new earth. Peter is saying that because of your relationship with God through Jesus, you have a share in the world that God is going to bring about when Jesus returns. It will be a world free of decay, destruction, death, and untouched by sin and suffering and never diminishing in its beauty or brightness. Everything that opposes the new world will be crushed under Jesus's feet. "The kingdom of the world has become the kingdom of our Lord and of his Christ, and he shall reign forever and ever" (Rev. 11:15). At the coming of Jesus, all things will be made new, and those who faithfully followed Jesus in the face of discrimination, prejudice, ridicule, mockery, risk, and loss will find eternal relief and reward in his presence.

According to 1 Peter 1:7 the trials and social alienation that we experience for our faith serve to prove the genuineness of our faith. They reveal that we are not fake or fair-weather fans of Jesus but truly are God's people who love and trust Christ. And these trials are winning for us the acclaim and praise of Jesus at his coming, which is stunning. When Peter says that "the tested genuineness of your faith . . . may be found to result in praise and glory and honor at the revelation of Jesus Christ," he is saying that you and your faith will receive commendation from Jesus when he visibly takes center stage and sets the world right. You will be praised and honored by him. You will have glory bestowed upon you.

The glory you have always wanted deep down, the compliments you have craved, and the recognition you have desired after every accomplishment are all just misdirected efforts to assuage a God-given ache to be spoken well of by him. We can have that. For those who hold on, who keep faith even through the fire of testing and affliction, who bear the reproach of Jesus and leverage their lives for his mission, an acclaim awaits them that is above all other acclaim. Every time you gladly and faithfully take it on the chin for Jesus, he sees and smiles and stores up acclaim for you. Every time you serve, sacrifice, and press on in the face of painful trials or difficult circumstances and no one applauds you or takes notice, he takes notice and will publicly notice you on that day.

Our hope—the great renewal and reward at Jesus's coming—the future orientation of our faith, is a part of our Christian living that I believe is greatly missing in the comfortable West. We so love this world, with all its shallow pleasures and delights and amenities, that we have killed our capacity to find deep joy in the world that is coming. This is also why so few of us are willing to sacrifice greatly or suffer rejection for our faith. We don't live with the coming world burning in our hearts. We rarely live with radical generosity and simplicity and boldness and abandon. We are slow to take great risk or put our reputation at stake for the sake of Jesus and his gospel because we live as if this world is all there is. Only the people who live with the world to come and the future reward of his acclaim burning in their hearts have their affections for this world broken. Only those who live with a real anticipation of his vindication are willing to risk losing face and place for his fame and mission. This is what Jesus meant when he said:

> Blessed are you when people hate you and when they exclude you and revile you and spurn your name as evil, on account of the Son of Man! Rejoice in that day, and leap for joy, for behold, your reward is great in heaven; for so their fathers did to the prophets. (Luke 6:22–23)

The words Jesus uses to describe people's actions toward the faithful are everything the glory hungry fear: being hated, excluded, reviled, and having their reputation soiled and spurned. But Jesus says that is reason not for shame but for celebration. It is an occasion to rejoice, to leap and dance for joy, because being temporarily shamed for Jesus in this world means being eternally celebrated by Jesus in the world to come.

We don't want to act as though the rejection of others doesn't hurt. Jesus knows it does. He has been there. And Peter knows it does. He has been there, too. That is why Peter says that we rejoice with joy inexpressible and filled with glory, even though for now we have to be grieved by various trials (1 Pet. 1:6, 8). We face some real pain and sorrow and cost and risk and loss in this broken world, especially for following Jesus. But the hope of his return, renewing all things and rewarding us, gives us an inexpressible joy that sustains us. What's at the end of our race sustains us in the race. Jesus is our ultimate example:

> Therefore, since we are surrounded by so great a cloud of witnesses, let us also lay aside every weight, and sin which clings so closely, and let us run with endurance the race that is set before us, looking to Jesus, the founder and perfecter of our faith, who for the joy that was set before him endured the cross, despising the shame, and is seated at the right hand of the throne of God. (Heb. 12:1–2)

Hebrews 12:1–2 may be a familiar passage, but don't let it be lost on you. For the joy set before him, Jesus endured the cross. There was a prize at the end of his race. He was exalted at the Father's right hand, his preincarnate glory restored. He was given all authority and dominion and power. His enemies are becoming his footstool. And he secured us as a prize, a people for his own possession. Because of this joy, the Scripture says he "despised the shame." The word translated "despise" means "to consider something not important enough to be an object of concern when evaluated against something else; to care nothing for, disregard."[32] So when measured against the gain of the cross, the joy at the end, the shame and agony of the cross seemed unimportant, insignificant, and of little concern.

There is a promised outcome that enables us to regard a cross and a crucifixion as insignificant. Hope fuels endurance and helps us to despise our present sufferings and inglorious treatment from people—not despise them in the sense of hating them but in the sense of seeing them as of little concern. To despise them is to mock them.

Hope enables us to look suffering and persecution in the eye and mock them. We say to risk and loss and ridicule and inglorious treatment from others, "You are grieving me, but you are also gaining for me a prize. So do your worst! Your days are numbered, and you are trivial when measured up against what awaits me." All that God *is* for me in this, and all that God *has* for me at the end will make all that I experience in the midst of this seem light and momentary.

Peter invites us to live fully for what is coming: "Set your hope fully on the grace that will be brought to you at the revelation of Jesus Christ" (1 Pet. 1:13). History is moving in a direction—the second coming of Jesus Christ. For those who know Jesus, that will be the full realization of all the grace that God can lavish on us. All things will be made new. Every cruel enemy that seeks to rise up over God and humiliate his people will be brought down. We will be raised up and fully transformed. Death will be destroyed, and the song of the ruthless will be put down. The people of God will be vindicated, and every tear will be wiped away. The faithful will receive their commendation and reward from Jesus: "Well done, good and faithful servant. . . . Enter into the joy of your master" (Matt. 25:21). It will be a never-ending happy ending.

Peter says the way you endure suffering is to live with the end in mind. Every sacrifice and all cost, risk, and loss will be infinitely comforted and turned to your eternal good. So, Peter says, live for that. Don't compromise your faith and live for momentary comfort. Don't hide in the shadows. Don't play it socially safe. Pay the cost of faith and live for eternal commendation. The end makes everything in the middle seem light and momentary.

A Pastoral Application

The eternal honor and reward that the apostle Peter speaks about is not for everyone. Peter makes that clear:

> So the honor is for you who believe, but for those who do not believe, "The stone that the builders rejected has become the cornerstone," and "A stone of stumbling, and a rock of offense." They stumble because they disobey the word, as they were destined to do. (1 Pet. 2:7–8)

There are real and lasting consequences to our response to Jesus. Peter cites Isaiah 8:14, which describes Jesus as the stone of stumbling and the rock of offense, by which Peter means that Jesus is an occasion for sin. Here is the point: Jesus presents us with the opportunity to experience the greatest rescue, a rescue from sin and judgment into the promise of glory. And he presents us with the opportunity for the greatest ruin. We can experience the greatest salvation or commit the greatest sin, that of rejecting the precious and chosen Son of God. God means for his Son, the chosen and precious cornerstone, to be polarizing. Jesus made that clear when he said:

> Do not think that I have come to bring peace to the earth. I have not come to bring peace, but a sword. For I have come to set a man against his father, and a daughter against her mother, and a daughter-in-law against her mother-in-law. And a person's enemies will be those of his own household. Whoever loves father or mother more than me is not worthy of me, and whoever loves son or daughter more than me is not worthy of me. (Matt. 10:34–37)

Jesus draws clear lines, and sometimes those lines divide even a household. Where loyalties conflict, Jesus demands that he take priority. Our post-Christian context has awakened us again to his polarizing nature. We can come to him for rescue or stumble over him to our ruin. We can embrace him and know his salvation, or we can take offense at him and reject him to our shame. Peter makes clear that to believe in him, to come to him, and to receive him mean honor (2:7). We will be honored by God as those who honor his Son. But to stumble over him, to take offense at him, to disobey this word of the gospel, and to reject him ultimately mean shame for us. A happy ending or a tragic ending.

If anyone is qualified to talk about these things, it's Peter. He stumbled along the way, denying Jesus three times during Jesus's arrest and trial. He chose to avoid the public shame of identifying with Jesus, only to weep bitterly over it in the end. After his resurrection, Jesus graciously restored Peter and recommissioned him to preach his gospel and lead his people. After the ascension, the Holy Spirit was sent upon the church, Peter boldly preached the gospel, and over three thousand people believed and were baptized. The rest of Peter's ministry is filled with preaching, imprisonment, miracles, and eventually martyrdom. Peter felt the pain of denying Jesus, and he felt the pain of publicly aligning with Jesus. One left him weeping bitterly; the other left him rejoicing with joy inexpressible and full of glory (1 Pet. 1:8).

When we see how the Father has vindicated the Son, sided with him and endorsed him in the resurrection, and exalted him to the highest place, giving him all dominion and authority, we see that the Christian life is a continual siding with Jesus against everything that competes with or contradicts him. In an emerging post-Christian context, to be a disciple of Jesus means we side with Jesus against the popular voices of culture. We share God's evaluation of the Son and highly esteem him above everything the culture esteems. We side with Jesus against even ourselves, choosing to deny our glory-hunger impulses toward reputation management, popularity, approval, and acceptance, and we gladly choose to honor the Son in keeping with his worth and preeminence.

That will certainly mean a measure of shame and rejection for us now; you can count on it. You can be sure that if you side with

Jesus you will be labeled, taunted, and condemned to the lower rungs of the cultural caste system. Your need for the immediate gratification of your glory hunger has to be renounced if you are going to side with Jesus. It will be eternally gratified when he bestows honor on you before men and angels. But in God's economy, when it comes to honor and shame, you get to choose one now and the other later. You can have honor now and, by denying Christ, spare a blow to your reputation and social clout, but you will have shame later. Or you can embrace shame now, siding with Jesus, but you will have honor later. Be careful here, because the one you choose to have later will be yours forever.

8

Glory Next Door

Talking about our glory hunger is tricky. As we have seen, the Scriptures clearly teach that in the end, the Father will be glorified in the exaltation of Jesus. At that time, Jesus will take center stage with no competitors. His name is the highest name, and everyone, even those who pierced him, will acknowledge his supremacy. This humbles us and decimates our narcissistic ambitions for recognition and praise. We don't want to find ourselves going against the grain of the universe and suffering humiliation in the end, yet the Bible is also clear that Jesus is committed to glorifying us. He is unwavering in his commitment to make us glorious. He promises an incomparable glory to those who love him and are faithful to him.

This theme of glory is a thread that runs through the entire fabric of the believer's life. In Jesus we have the present glory of the justifying verdict of God, his declaration of approval and acceptance. With that standing, we are given the glorious status of sons and daughters, fully and forever loved by the Father apart from our performance. We are known and cherished by the ultimate person. We are increasing in glory as we are made more like Jesus. The glorious image of God that was defaced by sin is being renewed and put on display in and through us. Day by day, Jesus is bringing out his likeness in us by the power of his Holy Spirit so that we are changed from one degree of glory to the next (2 Cor. 3:18).

Jesus's passion to make us glorious will be consummated at

his return. We will be "glorified with him" (Rom. 8:17), our lowly bodies being transformed and made "like his glorious body" (Phil. 3:21). "When he appears, we will appear with him in glory" (Col. 3:4). The purpose of the gospel is that we might "obtain the glory of the Lord Jesus" (2 Thess. 2:14). God destined us for this glory (Rom. 9:23). One day, at Jesus's return, we will "shine like the sun" in our Father's kingdom (Matt. 13:43), once again possessing the greatness God intended for humanity. All the shame that we might have encountered here while faithfully loving and serving Jesus will be wiped out, and we will be vindicated, sharing in Jesus's glory (1 Pet. 5:10). Our faithfulness to Jesus, though tested by trial and by inglorious treatment at the hands, swords, and pens of fallen people, will be celebrated by the Father and rewarded by the Son forever (1 Pet. 1:7). Eternal reward is stored up for those who invest in advancing the fame of Jesus at the cost of cultural infamy.

All your desire to shine, your passion for greatness, your longing for beauty, your wanting to win, your ache for affirmation, and your hunger for health and wholeness are clues to what you were made for. Sin can twist those desires, but they tell us something about our origin and intended destiny. They are like a homing device guiding us to Jesus, who alone can ultimately secure those things for us. So the Scriptures warn us not to seek glory from glory-hungry people, because it is a fading, temporary glory that will prove vain and disappointing in the end. The Bible motivates us to satiate our glory hunger in the right way, seeking glory from the glorious Father by responding to Jesus with everything we have.

In light of the promises, it appears that we have a smaller appetite for glory than we'd originally thought. We have been offered the stunning opportunity to be on a first-name basis with the Creator of heaven and earth. God has put before us the promise of possessing unspeakable beauty and unfading glory in an unshakable kingdom. He promises to us an eternal acclaim that will allay all the shame heaped upon us by powerful people who currently control the social currency. He has promised to make every loss for his name less than a memory in light of the irrevocable and indestructible treasure he has prepared for us. Yet we regularly prefer to play it safe, protecting our personal feelings from the rejection and ridicule of others, because the glory that comes from men means much more than the glory that comes from God. We are fools feasting on the wrong food.

Real, lasting, satisfying glory awaits, yet we prefer the gruel of people's praise. God must wake us up to our folly and open our eyes to what awaits the unashamed, those passionate for the renown of Jesus and ready to suffer any loss for the sake of his glory and future reward. If we could feel the weight of the glory that awaits us, we could finally feel the lightness of any shame or suffering we fear now. A vision of the glory to be revealed can liberate us from the glory hunger that keeps us quiet and cowering in an often hostile world that needs to be confronted with the love and lordship of Jesus.

Lest we think that our only motivation is our eternal glory in the end, we need to once again look to Jesus. While Jesus was on earth, he longed to glorify the Father and return to his Father and to the glory that he had before the world began (John 17:5). But he did not want to return alone. He told his disciples, "Truly, truly, I say to you, unless a grain of wheat falls into the earth and dies, it remains alone; but if it dies, it bears much fruit" (John 12:24). Jesus was willing to die so that we could see and share in his glory (John 17:24). He suffered that he might "bring many sons to glory" (Heb. 2:10). This was the purpose of his incarnation and his humiliation at the cross. Just as Jesus's focus on glorifying the Father reorients our life toward worship, Jesus's focus on bringing others into a share of his glory should also reorient us toward love, service, and mission. When we see Jesus suffering to secure our glory, we are free to seek glory for others instead of from them. Lewis is again helpful:

> It may be possible for each to think too much of his own potential glory hereafter; it is hardly possible for him to think too often or too deeply about that of his neighbour. The load, or weight, or burden of my neighbour's glory should be laid on my back, a load so heavy that only humility can carry it, and the back of the proud will be broken. It is a serious thing to live in a society of possible gods and goddesses, to remember that the dullest and most uninteresting person you can talk to may one day be a creature which, if you saw it now, you would be strongly tempted to worship, or else a horror and a corruption such as you now meet, if at all, only in a nightmare. All day long we are, in some degree, helping each other to one or other of these destinations. It is in the light of these overwhelming possibilities, it is with the awe and the circumspection proper to them, that we should conduct all our dealings with one another, all friendships, all loves, all play, all politics. There are no ordinary people. You have never talked to a mere mortal . . . it is immortals whom we joke with, work with, marry, snub and exploit. . . . Next to the blessed Sacrament itself, your neighbour is the holiest object presented to your senses.[33]

How often do you think about your neighbor's glory? The person across the street and the person across the ocean are destined for either eternal glory or eternal shame. Has that recently crossed your mind and sent you into prayer and action? To be rightly glory hungry means that we seek glory for the Father, and we seek glory from the Father, and we seek glory for our neighbor.

Jesus lived and died that way. He sought to glorify the Father in all things. He did all that was in the Father's heart for him to do out of love and submission to the Father. Jesus also sought glory from the Father. He was hungry for the glory that would come from pleasing the Father and being vindicated in his resurrection and exaltation. But Jesus was also hungry for your glory. He was willing to fall to the earth and die so that you could be where he is. He did not want this glory all to himself. At the cross Jesus suffered an inglorious ending to his life to secure a glorious ending for us. Now he has made us grains of wheat. In an infinitely lesser way, we too must fall to the ground and die, extending the gospel so that others might experience life.

Think of how radically different your life would look if you stopped seeking glory from people and started seeking glory for them. Think of how your life would look if Jesus was enough for you, and from his fullness you steadily received grace upon grace (John 1:16), satisfying your heart so you did not need anyone else to satisfy your heart. Think of the freedom that would come to you to serve the needs of others because you had been freed from needing others. When we are hungry for the glory that comes from people, we will use them, and we cannot properly love people whom we are using.

The apostle Paul reflected this attitude of Jesus consistently in his relationships. In his second letter to his protégé Timothy, Paul wrote:

> I am suffering, bound with chains as a criminal. But the word of God is not bound! Therefore I endure everything for the sake of the elect, that they also may obtain the salvation that is in Christ Jesus with eternal glory. (2 Tim. 2:9–10)

Paul, near the end of his life, imprisoned for the gospel, says, "I'm gladly enduring this so others can obtain eternal glory." Like the one who saved him, he was willing to suffer to bring others into the glory of being sons and daughters of God with the hope of eternal life.

On his second missionary journey, Paul planted the church in Thessalonica. After suffering in Philippi and being treated shamefully, Paul and his companions came to Thessalonica and preached the gospel there amidst much conflict (1 Thess. 2:2–3). Due to intense opposition he was forced to leave after only a short time. As Paul writes his first letter to them, his love and his passion for their life and joy in Christ come out clearly. He constantly thanks God for them (1:2) and recalls his ministry among them. You can hear his heart as he recalls how he and his team were gentle among them, "like a nursing mother taking care of her own children" (2:7). Not only did the apostles share with them the gospel, but they were ready to share their own lives because the people had become so dear to them, holding a special place in their hearts (2:8). They exhorted these new believers like a father would his children, encouraging them with the promise of glory and charging them to walk in a way that would honor God (1:11–12). Paul and his companions had a pure desire to see them experience God's grace and glory and were willing to suffer physical persecution and shame to see it happen. The key to that kind of posture is found in 2:4–6, where Paul writes:

> Just as we have been approved by God to be entrusted with the gospel, so we speak, not to please man, but to please God who tests our hearts. For we never came with words of flattery, as you know, nor with a pretext for greed—God is witness. Nor did we seek glory from people, whether from you or from others, though we could have made demands as apostles of Christ.

Because Paul was not seeking glory from them, he could seek glory for them. Paul did not need to make demands to be honored, respected, or even compensated, because he was finding his approval and security in God and his promises. Content as one loved by God, approved by God, entrusted by God with the gospel, and promised future reward, he was free to renounce concerns for his reputation and comfort, able to risk both to give the gospel to people who needed it. The path of demanding glory from others and the path of desiring glory for others produce two different kinds of lives.

I have discovered in my own life that my failures to truly love people and to be willing to sacrifice for them have been because I wanted more from them than I wanted for them. I was confronted by this ugly tendency in church planting. I had left a healthy church and moved to a new city, and I was expected to plant a successful church. When we started gathering people, and some other believers were joining our work, I was faced with the constant temptation to use them to make me a successful church planter. I felt that if the church failed, I would be a failure. My sense of worth was riding on this. I needed the church to make it so I could say that I had made it. This led me to make demands of people and place on them huge expectations. I was using them to build up my ministry instead of using my ministry to build them up. Instead of asking how I could best serve the people and their families, I found myself often asking what they could do to move the church forward. I believe that as a church planter and pastor, I did need to exhort them to give themselves to the work of the Lord, but for their joy and progress in the faith, not for my record as a church planter. God was gracious to show this to me and give me a great community that would forgive me and help me be a better pastor.

Even for those who know Jesus, using people is a constant temptation. We can desire respect and acceptance from the world more than we want God's heart for the world. The times I have chosen silence when I should have shared the gospel with another have often come from a desire for glory from them more than a glory for them. When I have failed to confront another believer who is in error doctrinally or morally, it is because I have wanted not to come across as judgmental or critical. I have sought to preserve my image to them instead of pursuing God's image formed in them. When I have held on to my resources instead of releasing them for God's mission, it is because I have wanted glory for myself in the form of comfort and the reputation derived from possessions more than I have wanted glory for the unreached and oppressed.

The failure to love is wanting more for ourselves than we want for others. When we want glory for ourselves and seek it from others more than we want glory for others, we lose the power to make a difference in the lives of others. We will never fall to the earth and die when we are asking everyone else to prop us up. If we live that way, the tragedy is that we remain by ourselves; we will not live fruitful lives and leave a legacy of kingdom impact. But if we care less about our reputation and comfort, and care more for God's fame and his purposes in the lives of people, we will choose to lose so others can gain.

A Final Appeal

The world needs glory-hungry men and women—but not insecure, glory-hungry men and women who are always fretting over what people think about them; not the glory-hungry men and women who strut in pride and narcissism, promoting and serving themselves; not glory-hungry men and women who exert their energy climbing ladders and spending their time and money accruing clout. We have enough of that in this world. We need men and women who are hungry for the glory that comes from God. This world needs a generation that is satisfied with God's acceptance of them in Jesus; a multitude of people who are happy with and confident in the justifying verdict of God over their lives; men and women who revel in God's unreserved *yes* spoken over them in Christ and who can risk the world's *no*. The world needs men and women who no longer live to please others—an impossible folly—but men and women who live for the Lord's pleasure and are content with his "very good" ringing in their ears.

We need glory-hungry men and women who seek glory for the triune God. We need a groundswell of saints, smitten with the beauty and power of God, who refuse to compete with him for praise. We don't lack for glory-hungry men and women who snap selfies and yell, "Look at me!" This world is heavy on those who can't see that there is something heavier to love and live for. We need the heart of the psalmist who prays, "Not to us, O Lord!" We need the glory hunger of Jesus that cries, "Father, glorify your name!" We need men and women dialed into the preeminence of Jesus and can clearly see the end of all glories raised up against his. We need men and women who have stopped selling tickets to their own show and are praying for Jesus to take center stage and set the world right.

We need glory-hungry people who seek glory for others and not for themselves. This world needs men and women who love most what is most lovely, and who can fearlessly invite their neighbors to reorient their lives toward ultimate reality and move in step with the course of the universe. The call goes out for men and women who, with humble love, are willing to suffer any shame so that the nations might obtain eternal glory. God is looking for men and women who will go across the street or across an ocean so that others can share in the surpassing glory that will one day be revealed. The world needs people who are fixed on the promises of God and are not afraid of the threats of mere men. The world may not know it, but it is desperate for Christians who will bear the reproach of Christ so that others might be made partakers of his glory. The need of the hour is followers of Jesus Christ who will take it on the chin, faithfully telling the world of his greatness, looking to that glorious day when he will honor them with praise.

May we who have come to live under the affirmation of our God and Father, and who are zealous for his honor among all peoples, gladly give ourselves to his mission, risking the status of outcast so that others might be brought into the enjoyment of his grace and glory now and forevermore. And as we ready ourselves to lose the glory that comes from men, may we love and eagerly anticipate the glory that comes from God. Amen.

Acknowledgments

Speaking of seeking glory for others, I have many to thank for the kindness, support, and generosity shown to me during this process. Thank you, Apostles Church NYC, for teaching me how to be a pastor and for loving me and being patient with me when I was not a good one. I'll always have you in my heart. Thank you, Matt Chandler, Josh Patterson, Michael Bleeker, and the community of the Village Church. You are a special people, and you have refreshed my soul more than once. Thank you, Crossway, for taking a chance on me and being patient with me through this process. You have been wonderful to work with. Thank you, Brandon O'Brien. There is no way in the cosmos I could have pulled this off without your feedback and counsel. Thank you, Jeff Willingham, for letting me write in your tire shop and hay field. You are a deacon and a friend. Thank you, Church at the Cross, for providing such a soft landing for our family as we reentered the Republic of Texas. I'm glad to be your pastor. Thank you, Gene and Gloria, for being amazing in-laws and giving our family a place to rest and taking such good care of your kids. And, lastly, thank you, Ginger, Neeley, Judson, and Korey. Next to Jesus, you are the most glorious thing in my life.

Notes

1. J. R. R. Tolkien, *The Lord of the Rings* (London: HarperCollins, 2005), Kindle edition, 18,529–18,531.
2. C. S. Lewis, *The Weight of Glory* (San Francisco: HarperCollins, 2001), 147–48.
3. Edward T. Welch, *When People Are Big and God Is Small: Overcoming Peer Pressure, Codependency, and the Fear of Man* (Phillipsburg, NJ: P&R, 1997), 13.
4. Breeanna Hare, "Donald Glover, and 15 More Stars on Fear and Insecurity," *CNN Entertainment*, http://www.cnn.com/2013/10/16/showbiz/celebrity-news-gossip /insecure-celebrities-donald-glover/index.html (accessed January 21, 2014).
5. Ibid.
6. Ibid.
7. Philip Schaff, *The Creeds of Christendom, with a History and Critical Notes: The Evangelical Protestant Creeds, with Translations*, vol. 3 (New York: Harper & Brothers, 1882), 327.
8. Lewis, *Weight of Glory*, 38–39.
9. Thomas J. Egger, "Jesus: The Second and Greater Adam," *Modern Reformation* 22 (November–December, 2013): 44.
10. Tears for Fears, "Everybody Wants to Rule the World," *Songs from the Big Chair*, producer Chris Hughes (Somerset, UK: Mercury, 1985).
11. Egger, "Jesus: The Second and Greater Adam," 42.
12. C. S. Lewis, *Prince Caspian: The Return to Narnia* (New York: HarperCollins, 2008), Kindle edition, 2,176–2,178.
13. Jean Twenge, *The Narcissism Epidemic* (New York: Simon & Schuster, 2009), Kindle edition, 239.
14. Ibid., 249.
15. Mark Sayers, *The Vertical Self: How Biblical Faith Can Help Us Discover Who We Are in an Age of Self Obsession* (Nashville: Thomas Nelson, 2010), Kindle edition, 34.
16. Twenge, *Narcissism Epidemic*, 2,555.
17. Ibid., 1,603.
18. Sayers, *Vertical Self*, 34.
19. Sarah Kessler, "What Would You Say to a Million Twitter Users? Fame Hopes to Find Out," *Mashable.com*, March 27, 2012, http://mashable.com/2012/03/27/twitter -fame/ (accessed January 21, 2014).
20. Eugene Peterson, *Where Your Treasure Is: Psalms That Summon You from Self to Community* (Grand Rapids, MI: Eerdmans, 1993), 12.

21. David K. Naugle, *Reordered Love, Reordered Lives: Learning the Deep Meaning of Happiness* (Grand Rapids, MI: Eerdmans, 2008), Kindle edition, 648–52.

22. Taken from the subtitle of Peterson's *Where Your Treasure Is: Psalms That Summon You from Self to Community.*

23. Stephen Charnock, *The Existence and Attributes of God*, vol. 2 (Grand Rapids, MI: Baker, 1996), 360.

24. John Calvin, *Institutes of the Christian Religion*, trans. Henry Beveridge (Bellingham, WA: Logos Bible Software, 1997), 1.1.3.

25. John Piper, *Don't Waste Your Life* (Wheaton, IL: Crossway, 2003), 163.

26. Naugle, *Reordered Love*, 205.

27. John R. W. Stott, *The Message of Galatians*, The Bible Speaks Today (Downers Grove, IL: InterVarsity, 1984), electronic ed., 179.

28. S. P. Sullivan, "By the Numbers: A Brief History of Blue Laws in Bergen," *NJ.com*, http://www.nj.com/bergen/index.ssf/2012/11/by_the_numbers_a_brief_history_of _blue_laws_in_bergen_county.html (accessed January 21, 2014).

29. Stanley Hauerwas and William Willimon, *Resident Aliens: A Provocative Christian Assessment of Culture and Ministry for People Who Know That Something Is Wrong* (Nashville: Abingdon, 1989), 15.

30. Ibid., 15–17.

31. "Religious Hostilities Reach Six-Year High," Pew Forum, January 14, 2014, http:// www.pewforum.org/2014/01/14/religious-hostilities-reach-six-year-high/ (accessed January 23, 2014).

32. William Arndt, Frederick W. Danker, and Walter Bauer, *A Greek-English Lexicon of the New Testament and Other Early Christian Literature* (Chicago: University of Chicago Press, 2000), s.v. "despise."

33. Lewis, *Weight of Glory*, 45–46.

General Index

Scripture Index

Download a free study guide

for *Glory Hunger* at

crossway.org/GloryHungerSG